ONE CHURCH: CATHOLIC AND REFORMED

Books by Lewis S. Mudge

Published by The Westminster Press

One Church: Catholic and Reformed

In His Service

ONE CHURCH: CATHOLIC AND REFORMED

Toward a Theology for Ecumenical Decision

by

1344

LEWIS S. MUDGE

THE WESTMINSTER PRESS
PHILADELPHIA

First published 1963
Library of Congress Catalog Card No. 63-11561

PRINTED IN GREAT BRITAIN

INTRODUCTION

Dr. Mudge's volume, ONE CHURCH: CATHOLIC AND REFORMED, has grown out of a study of "Catholicity" that was undertaken by the Department of Theology of the World Alliance of Reformed and Presbyterian Churches at the request of its Executive Committee. While working papers have been circulated and have received the most widespread and thorough criticism, the present study is the work of the author and reflects his own contribution to the ongoing quest among the churches for the nature of the unity which Christ wills for His Church.

It would be difficult to select another period in the history of the Church when such a study would have been more urgent and more relevant. For centuries we have confessed our faith according to the Apostles' Creed, although each tradition has had its own peculiar way or ways of interpreting the article, "I believe in the Holy Catholic Church." For one it meant the unbroken tradition of the undivided Church, for another being in communion with Rome, for another one or more versions of episcopacy, and for others allegiance to a confession.

The situation among the churches today, however, has been radically altered, as the Holy Spirit has used the ecumenical movement to break down barriers that have separated traditions and confirmed churches in their insularity and parochialism. We are in the happy position of recognizing that while discussions have been taking place and agreements have been sought, more often than not vainly, God has done something in our midst. An atmosphere has been created, a climate has developed, in which separated communions can now talk together within a new context.

This new context for ecumenical discussion and decision was first recognized in 1952 when the Faith and Order Conference was convened in Lund. It was a milestone in that it marked the end of the method of comparative ecclesiology, by which each tradition simply tried to explain its own position as clearly as possible. The new factor was the growing awareness of a common tradition, shared by all but possessed by none. With this awareness another shift became evident. It would no longer be possible to discuss catholicity in terms that are merely historical or geographical, for history has many skeins and our geographies overlap and compete. Another dimension has come to the fore, the eschatological, where the fulness or plenitude of the Church is sought in the continuing redemptive work of the Triune God and in the Church's becoming a fitter instrument for her Head.

This is not to say that history has ceased to be important or that it is not being corrected. It is notoriously true, for example, that something happened to Roman Catholicism and to Protestantism in the sixteenth century as each attempted to define its position. In each case the definition tended to be negative. At the Council of Trent the Roman Church formed its decrees against the doctrines of the Reformation, while the Reformation doctrines were drawn up against the unscriptural superstitions of late medieval Romanism, with the result that both traditions have come down to the twentieth century doctrinally impaired and impoverished.

The extent to which the situation has changed may be seen in the reassessment of the Reformation by Catholic historians like Josef Lortz and Pierre Janelle and in the theological writings of a Catholic theologian like Hans Küng. On the Protestant side similar reappraisals are in progress, although it is lamentably true that the results have not yet begun to penetrate the broad spectrum of Protestant church life and thought.

Moreover, the coming of Eastern Orthodoxy in such great strength into the World Council of Churches is one more evidence of how the Holy Spirit has broken down barriers of separation. Our most pressing challenge is to engage this historic tradition of Christendom in the sort of dialogue that will lead to deeper mutual understanding and mutual enrichment. Orthodoxy's staying power, its rich liturgical life, and its demonstrable capacity to hold the loyalty of the faithful against the greatest of obstacles are gifts that cannot be lightly dismissed, while Protestantism's capacity for self-criticism and insistence on the necessity of the Church's bringing her total life under the scrutiny and judgment of God's healing Word for correction and renewal are emphases that Orthodoxy will do well to examine closely. That this can now be done, naturally and without acrimonious debate, is a witness to the presence of the new context for ecumenical decision and to the growing quest for catholicity.

This new situation has not left Protestantism unaffected in its intra-mural relations. The Consultation on Church Union in the United States is an illustration of the willingness of six separated denominations to come together and to work responsibly toward creating a church that would be truly catholic, truly reformed, and truly evangelical. It should be made clear, though, that true catholicity, in the sense of the Church's fulness, will include that which is reformed and evangelical, for each emphasis developed historically in an attempt to lay fresh claim on the Word of the gospel. It was the historian, Philip Schaff, who reminded us that the Reformation was "a deeper plunge into the meaning of the gospel."

Dr. Mudge's study of catholicity has appeared at a time when another dramatic change is taking place in the life of the Church. This is being occasioned by a fresh look at the conciliar movement and by the posing of the question of the ecclesiological significance of councils of churches. Church councils have furnished the twentieth century's response to the ecumenical imperative. They have brought communions together for programs of service and witness, have provided a forum for conversations among divided brethren, and have been instruments of the church's renewal. The significance of the conciliar movement is emphatically great. But it has weaknesses inherent in its very nature. Co-operative Christianity is still divided Christianity, and a response limited to mere co-operation is too easy and too cheap. It does not require repentance, nor does it overcome the obstacles in the path of the Church's mission which our disunity erects.

The churches of the West are being summoned today to another and more costly response to the ecumenical imperative, and the younger churches will not remain content with our continued evasion of this demand. The bitter denunciation of world confessionalism by the East Asia Christian Conference in Bangalore in the fall of 1961 is indicative of the resentment which our artificial divisions have produced. They ask if we are willing to take seriously a commitment to unity that will challenge our separate traditions as together with Christians of widely diverse backgrounds and cultures we seek the fulness of Christ's Church; are we willing to pray "veni, Creator spiritus," if the Creator Spirit's coming will judge and destroy familiar structures in order to free the Church? are we willing to accept whatever the Spirit creates in our midst if it violates our reverence for the past? Today Protestantism is shackled with traditions. The very language the sixteenth century reformers used in their efforts to free the gospel from institutional domestication must now be directed against their sons who have made idols of Reformation traditions. This conviction is leading the churches to face frankly the question, what comes next? for they have traveled together in co-operation much too long to stop their journey at some halfway house.

Dr. Mudge, in dealing with the new context for ecumenical decision and with the new direction of the ecumenical imperative, writes as a Reformed churchman and theologian. The final chapter leaves no doubt on this score. He is fully aware that his own tradition has from its beginning claimed catholicity for itself, not exclusively but nonetheless genuinely. And he is no exponent of unity at any cost, especially if the price is theological irresponsibility and the level is that of a least common denominator. He also writes as one who has been intimately involved in the ecumenical movement and who is abreast of the best in current ecumenical thought. His study should be read widely and pondered deeply by Christians of all communions who seek to participate in the "great conversation" among the churches and to become involved in the quest for the unity which God has in store for His people.

JAS. I. McCORD

CONTENTS

ACKNOWLEDGMENTS

THIS BOOK is the product of more than the usual amount of conversation and consultation. That has been inevitable, in view of the volume's integral relationship with the catholicity study of the World Presbyterian Alliance. Furthermore, the very fact that the writing has been done at 17 Route de Malagnou, Geneva, the headquarters of the World Council of Churches as well as of the Alliance, has made it possible to be in touch with a large number of people who know a great deal about the subject, and who have taken a warm interest in this attempt to put some thoughts concerning it on paper.

It would be impossible to list everyone who has had some part, direct or indirect, in helping the writer to formulate his ideas. Those mentioned here, however, have been of substantial aid. It goes without saying, of course, that they are not responsible for the result. Among the participants in the catholicity study whose work has been notably helpful have been Hendrik Berkhof, Thomas F. Torrance, Elton Eenigenburg and John Newton Thomas. Chapter drafts were read and criticized by Paul Minear, Lukas Vischer, and Lesslie Newbigin. The whole has benefited from the constant yet discriminating encouragement of James I. McCord and the writer's successor in the Alliance Department of Theology, Terrence Tice. A special debt of gratitude goes to Rosemarie Müller, who cheerfully typed and re-typed the manuscript in its various stages.

LEWIS S. MUDGE

1

TOWARD A THEOLOGY FOR ECUMENICAL DECISION

IN HIS book, *The Pressure of Our Common Calling*,[1] Dr. W. A. Visser't Hooft calls for a theology of the way unity *grows*. He writes:

> We have a wealth of literature on the issues of church unity, but this deals nearly exclusively with the question: What are the true characteristics of a united Church? Now this is obviously a fundamental problem ... but it is not the only ecumenical problem ... A theology of the ecumenical movement must deal with the meaning of our *present* relationships. It must give guidance for that in-between period when we can no longer remain wholly isolated from each other ... but when we are not yet able to enter into that full fellowship ... which would express itself in living together as members of one visible body (p. 14).

Dr. Visser't Hooft goes on to point out that this is not merely a question to be dealt with within the World Council of Churches. The need for a theology of growing unity

> applies equally to the various bodies which together make up the ecumenical movement. In this matter there is no fundamental difference between the tasks of the World Council of Churches, of the International Missionary Council, of the confessional alliances, and of the "independent" Christian lay movements (p. 15).

The "in-between" period of which the General Secretary of the World Council of Churches speaks is likely to be with us for a long time. The most comprehensive unity schemes have, to

[1] Doubleday, New York 1959; S.C.M. Press, London.

date, involved only a few of the many confessions and communions of Christendom. Conversations with the Roman Catholic Church, which perhaps will eventually raise the most profound questions of all, are still in their infancy. Thus, the need for a theological understanding of our present interchurch relationships is vital, not only for charting a course towards a unity which we cannot yet fully describe, but for living together as creatively and imaginatively as possible in the present generation.

Moreover, Dr. Visser't Hooft is surely correct in insisting that dealing with this question is everyone's responsibility. If unity is to grow, churches, communions and confessions must decide to move. How are they to make the fateful decisions required of them? Who will take the responsibility for such decisions, and on what authority? Ultimately the responsibility is placed, not on the secretariat of the World Council or any other ecumenical organization, but on the leadership of the church bodies involved. Dr. Visser't Hooft's plea can therefore be sharpened. We need not only a theology of how unity grows. We need, in every church, a theology of ecumenical *decision*. A church must know its reasons for moving. It must not hold back when every theological consideration calls for action. It must not act for reasons unworthy of its deepest understanding of the gospel.

These are the thoughts which have prompted the study of which this book is a result. There is surely no higher ecumenical loyalty than the determination to wrestle with what one's own church, and others of like confession, must do as a consequence of their ecumenical commitment. The Reformed churches, which include virtually all which use the name Presbyterian as well as like-minded bodies on the continent of Europe, have taken an extremely active part in ecumenical affairs. They have contributed numerous effective persons to the staffs of world church organizations. There are few union schemes of any importance in which they have not been involved. But long ecumenical experience and unwavering commitment to the goal of Christian unity have not, in themselves, solved every theological problem. It is probably not too much to say, indeed, that we are only now beginning to realize how theologically serious and complex the question of our participation in the ecumenical movement is.

The New Arena for Ecumenical Decision

The ecumenical movement is no longer (if it ever was) a pleasant little club in which church leaders of mainly Protestant persuasion can gather to discuss interminably their amiable differences. Providentially, it has become more than that. Consider such items as the following. For the first time in a thousand years, there is a chance of getting to work on the great schism between the churches of East and West. By a stroke of providence or by political circumstance, it is non-Roman Christendom which is given this opportunity to confront Eastern Orthodoxy at a profound theological level. Is the non-Roman Church of the West ready for this opportunity? Can Reformed churches be content to play anything but a major part in the theological task that must be accomplished? And what of the most portentous confrontation of all, with Roman Catholicism itself? Relations with Rome are beginning to influence the ecumenical scene, and will continue to do so. There are responsibilities and opportunities here that cannot be evaded.

Such responsibilities are thrust upon Protestantism, moreover, at a moment when existing union efforts, among churches of the non-Roman West and their offshoots, are not exhibiting much success. The ecumenical honeymoon, even leaving Rome and the Orthodox out of account, is over. We have been involved in union negotiations that have failed, or have been, for all intents and purposes, suspended. We are at present involved in several union projects that are in serious trouble. One of these, the Ceylon scheme, has been so widely copied that its failure would be likely to pull a host of other plans down with it. Who is responsible for these difficulties? There is the appearance of increasing denominational and confessional intransigence, coupled with growing unrest and lack of direction within the same denominational and confessional bodies. One is bound to ask whether one's own church has at times been guilty of non-theological obstructionism and plain theological incompetence. Is it possible that many unions, even among churches which have known each other for a long time, are not to be consummated without being reconsidered in the infinitely broader and more complex context afforded by the presence of Orthodoxy and Rome? From an ecumenical standpoint, indeed, may this not be theologically appropriate? But how great, then, is the amount of theological work yet to be done! And how weighty is the responsibility of each church for making the needed decisions!

The expanding significance of councils of churches, and particularly of the World Council, is also to be considered. For example, the growth of the World Council is bringing about a notable shift in the balance of confessional power within that organization. It is leading to profound changes in the character, training and commitments of ecumenical leadership. Most important of all, however, the question of what the Council is in itself becomes increasingly pressing. To what extent is the Council not merely a co-operative administrative agency but a work of the Holy Spirit in such a way that it ever more fully represents *in itself* the fellowship of the Una Sancta?

Questions such as these invite us to re-explore the basis on which we are part of the ecumenical movement, and the basis on which we make, or will make, decisions to move. Moreover, such questions demand genuinely *theological* grounds for ecumenical decision. But it is precisely this for which we are not prepared. Neither the traditional theologies of our churches nor the documents and pronouncements of ecumenical organizations sufficiently prepare us for it. We are living through one of the greatest periods of theological renewal in the history of the Church, and yet we have difficulty in bringing this new thinking to bear upon the actual ecclesiastical decisions we have to make. On the one hand, the official theological positions of the churches, those that are expressed in confessions of faith, built into structures of polity, or enshrined in liturgy, no longer wholly determine the way we actually live, particularly in matters of church administration at the denominational level. Often these traditional theological positions are not expressed in terminology directly applicable to our ecumenical situation. Yet unless we can appeal to them in some creative way, we find ourselves cast adrift from the past and unable to move *as churches* into new relationships. On the other hand, theological material from ecumenical sources is not yet ready to serve as a substitute for our traditional confessions of faith. A great deal of the theological achievement of the ecumenical movement has lain in the common discovery of God's gift of unity in Christ, comprehending and overruling our diversity. But this discovery has been confined too much to persons who have had the opportunity to participate in ecumenical meetings. It has not so far proved communicable in all its revolutionary implications. Too often, the result of ecumenical discussion has appeared to be a multitude of isolated *ideas*: methods for Bible study, new viewpoints concerning the laity, insights concerning the stance of the Church in the world. These ideas have been taken over by the churches as highly useful for "program planning", but it has not occurred to enough people that what lies behind the ideas might well challenge the confessional bases of the churches as such.

In short, our traditional positions and our ecumenical discoveries do not yet meet in revitalizing encounter. The area in which we live and act as churches is still too much a theological vacuum. In this vacuum we are trying to make decisions about our relations to other churches, and to the world. Such a basis for ecumenical decision is obviously not good enough. We do not plead for some new ecumenical scholasticism in which every step towards unity or renewal would be justified in exhausting detail. One is better off knowing where one has come from, where one hopes to go, and moving by faith in the meantime. But manifestly, however great our faith may be, in too many places we have been moving for inadequate reasons or not moving at all. A shaft of theological illumination on the meaning of movement will surely be welcome if it can be gained. And illumination certainly can be had if enough attention is given to this neglected area of ecumenical study.

The Theological Significance of the Interim

What ecumenical decision-making means would be clearer if we were able to make theological sense of the "in-between" situation in which we live. Let us begin by trying to describe the situation itself. We, the many "churches", have discovered, not just in theory but in fact, that there is such a thing as *the Church*. By the grace of God it has been given to us, acting together, to *be* the Church under certain circumstances. At ecumenical conferences, in common social action, in study, we have come to see that the Church of Jesus Christ is not an empty phrase but a reality that can exist on earth by the power of the Holy Spirit. No one of the ecclesiastical bodies we represent is the Church in itself, nor is the Church simply the sum total of denominations. The Church is something more. To be the Church is God's gift to us, and it is also the task which God sets before us. Our calling is to live as "churches" which acknowledge this gift and this task. This is our "in-between situation".

The discovery of the Church by the churches is a distinctive ecumenical experience. Concretely, the discovery has been made in a multitude of ways. It has been made at great assemblies, but also under more modest circumstances when Christians have so thought and acted as to fulfil the mission of the Church in some given situation. One thinks of such diverse examples as moments in the work of the French Protestant relief organization Cimade, or the high moment of courageous witness represented by the 1960 Cottesloe consultation on the churches and the problem of race in South Africa. A discovery of the Church, furthermore, has taken place in theological discussion. The Lutheran and Reformed theologians who met at Arnoldshain, Germany in 1957 to frame a joint statement on the Lord's Supper had the audacity to note in their preface that they wrote not as representatives of confessions but as theologians of the Church universal. In instances too numerous to number, indeed, Christian men and women have reached the point of asking the radical question: What does God demand that His Church be here and now? At that moment the "churches" discover the meaning of the Una Sancta, and become representatives of it in so far as they are obedient.

The fact that this possibility exists has worked a remarkable change in the standpoint from which churches may legitimately carry on their decision-making. When the various churches were isolated, they could think of themselves as fully and authentically churchly, if only because other Christian bodies did not seem to require any serious consideration. Today, churches must consider their reason for being on an entirely new basis. The ecumenical commitment does not call upon any church to relativize its claim to be the church of Jesus Christ where it lives and ministers. The idea that because a church participates in ecumenical relationships it should consider the truth it professes to be in some sense partial, has proved a blind alley. On the contrary, participation in the ecumenical movement underlines the responsibility of each church to *be* the Church of Jesus Christ in and through its existing forms. But now, and this is the great change that has come, one can see that one's own church can *be* the Church of Jesus Christ not because other churches, in effect, do not exist, but precisely because they do. A given church is the Church *because* of the *oikumene*, on behalf of it, and for it.

This means that a church, even though it may believe itself to be the only fully authentic manifestation of the Body of Christ, will yet realize that in every deed, sacramental or otherwise, it acts for the Una Sancta. The forms, the beliefs, and the customs of each church do duty in a given place for the whole of Christ's Church, which is present through those particular forms *there*. Our particular doctrines, whatever they may be, thus have a tremendous vicarious load to carry. Our church life is called upon to function ecumenically at all times, whether Christians of other confessions are present or not, because our ecumenical commitment has lifted everything we do into a new dimension. Whether our forms are inherently able to carry such a burden is a question which may eventually break them down or transform them. But such disintegration or change will not be an absorption of these forms into something else, or a denial of that for which they stand. If this picture is right, ecumenical change will be an affirmation of what our forms of life truly are intended to be: ordinances in which the whole Christ lives among His people and makes Himself known to them.

Thus our interim situation has a two-sided character. There is but one Church of Jesus Christ. We can never rest content until that one Church becomes a visible, living reality on earth. Yet, even in our existing divisions, each separate church must seek to *be* the Church in all possible fulness. It is surely wrong to argue from the fact that we are divided that our being-in-Christ is somehow diminished in character, intensity, or validity. Rather, there is a paradox to be maintained. We are either the Church of Jesus Christ or a congregation of Satan. No intermediate possibilities exist. Yet the Church *is* one, and we must never lose sight of the responsibility for growth and change this places upon us.

The tension involved in this situation is reflected in the double application of Paul's question "Is Christ divided?" This challenge to the Corinthian community speaks to us both as we are now and as we may be when we are one. The Greek here deserves careful exegesis. The term *memeristai*, which we translate "divided", means not merely "split", but also "distributed", "parcelled out", or "assigned". This, for example, is the meaning in I Cor. 7: 17: "Only let everyone lead the life which the Lord has assigned (*memeriken*) to him . . ." The fundamental point of I Cor. 1: 13 is, therefore, that there is no such thing as a partial Christ, a half-time Christ, or a diluted Christ. He is present or He is not, and there are no two ways about it.

Quite properly, we draw the conclusion from this that the Church is essentially one, that it cannot in principle be divided and still be the Church. But sometimes we fail to see that if the Church *is* divided in fact, the whole Christ must still be wherever the Church exists. It is utterly unscriptural to think of the divided parts of Christendom as in some sense less *fully* churchly than a united church would be, quite apart from the opening this provides for the claim that one church is fuller or less full in some respects than others. Where Jesus Christ is, there is the Church. The fulness towards which we move is an eschatological fulness, not a quantitative fulness. The real cutting edge of I Cor. 1:13 for separated churches in the throes of ecumenical decision is not that it encourages them to seek something "more" by union, but that it insists that they be faithful to the whole Christ who is already in them, seeking the further unity of the Church out of the power that He gives. In the *Cambridge New Testament* Parry translates this verse, "Has Christ shared you with others?" The implication, of course, is that a "partial" Christ is one we share with some other master. The real sin of the Church, divided or united, is idolatry: of human masters, of cultural surroundings, of the *status quo*, of dead tradition. Paul, Cephas, and Apollos did not divide Christ between them. They threatened to set themselves up in His place.

If the ecumenical situation is looked at in this perspective, much becomes clear. The discovery of the Church we have made in common is also a discovery about ourselves as churches. It is a discovery of what it means to say that God has *already* given us His Son, and that ecumenical decision is decision to be truly what we already are in principle. The ecumenical movement does not submerge churches in the bigness of a world enterprise which claims to do everything better and more authoritatively than it can be done by them. On the contrary, correctly understood, it lifts churches up, and shows them what they are. Human beings, after all, do not decide to change because they believe they are weak. They change because, in a more fundamental way, they are strong: because the roots of change are already in them, because it is in them to grow into something new. Churches, being human, are the same. The ecumenical interim in which we live has taught us the lesson that we *are* strong because Christ is in us. Out of what we are we must undertake the task of becoming what God wants us to be.

The Attribute of Catholicity

Obviously our understanding of the two-sided situation in which we stand needs to be carried still further. One way to do this may be to reopen the ancient and perennial question of the meaning of *catholicity*. This word has traditionally been used to denote the wholeness of the Church both in the sense of its *extension* through time and to the ends of the earth, and in the sense of its *authenticity* in terms of the gospel at any given moment or place. Any consideration we give to this concept will force us both to consider the fact that the Church *is* universal and to probe the status of our own particular church in relation to this wider reality.

The adjective *catholic*, of course, is one of the four "marks" of the Church mentioned in both the Nicene and Apostles' Creeds. The Church is said to be one, holy, and apostolic, as well as catholic. These terms are mutually interrelated in such a way that any one can carry most of the meaning of the others. The choice of one of them for special attention is more a matter of placing the total being of the Church in a certain light, of asking questions of a certain kind, than it is of dividing off a distinct and self-contained subject-matter for analysis. If catholicity is rightly seen, there will be no question but that it involves unity, holiness, and apostolic truth. But unity, holiness, and truth will be seen in the perspective of wholeness: wholeness of faith and wholeness of world involvement.

The word catholicity has achieved this richness of meaning in a gradual and still continuing process of semantic development. The term in the Creed is borrowed from the Greek, and means something which has the attribute of being *kath'holon*, total, or comprehending the whole. Until the present century the word has more often than not been understood by the Church at large in a quantitative, or geographical, sense. It has been used in the sense of the Vincentian Canon, "that which has been believed everywhere, always and by all", to denote that which has the authority of Christian usage in every time and place. Alternatively, it has been employed to indicate that the Church has spread over the whole earth, being called "out of every kindred, and tongue, and people, and nation" (Rev. 5: 9). The twentieth century, however, has taken a logical step from both these usages to a more qualitative, theological understanding.

This new understanding, of course, goes back to certain ancient roots. Cyril of Jerusalem and Augustine both were aware of a qualitative range of meaning in the term catholicity. But the modern usage of the word is a direct product of its involvement in ecumenical discussions. Theologians of different communions have sought to grasp the significance of the whole church, of the whole of God's action in the world, for their churches, and the significance of their own churches for the whole. This has led, particularly in Roman Catholic, Anglican, and certain Lutheran circles, to a series of varying attempts to ask in what sense these churches possess the *essence* of what makes the Church the Church. To a large degree, the question of catholicity has thus become What? rather than Where? What is *the* mark of real churchliness *because* it is found among authentic Christian believers of all ages and times? What ecclesiastical or theological factor determines whether Christ's people does exist at a given place or time?

One must reckon, for example, with Yves Congar's *Chrétiens Désunis* and *Catholicisme Hier, Aujourd'hui, Demain*.[1] Congar's work, a classic attempt to see his own church in the context of the Una Sancta, has had tremendous influence on the post-war "nouvelle théologie" within the church of Rome. For Congar the Church catholic is a oneness in diversity. Its unity is grounded in the unity of creation and redemption in Christ. Catholicity is precisely that attribute of the Church by virtue of which the fact of its diversity is fully reconciled with the equally given fact of its unity. This fulness is not completely worked out even in the

[1] I have made use of the excellent summary of Congar's views and their influence in Hendrik Berkhof's article "The Catholicity of the Church", *Bulletin* of the Department of Theology of the World Presbyterian Alliance, Vol. II, No. 2, Autumn 1961.

Roman Catholic Church. Non-Roman Christian bodies are regarded by Congar not as apostate communities but as "separated churches". They are stirred by authentic spiritual values, which values have the quality of catholicity even though they have been developed one-sidedly because they are outside the body of Christ. Such principles of the Reformation as *sola gratia* and *soli Deo gloria*, for example, are "values" which belong in the Church catholic, and which should once again be gathered into it. Such a gathering would mean the enrichment of the formerly separated brethren as well as of the Roman Church itself. Although Rome possesses all the "values" of faith in principle, Congar cautiously explains, without reunion it will continue to be unable to express its inherent catholicity fully.

On the Protestant side similar ideas have been influential in certain circles, particularly on the European Continent. The Swedish Lutheran Archbishop Söderblom popularized the expression "evangelical catholicity". He was followed in this by his friend Friedrich Heiler, first a Roman Catholic and then a Lutheran, who published a book under this title in 1926, and by the Dutch theologian Van der Leeuw. This "catholicizing" circle, like that of Congar and his followers, understood catholicity to mean mainly the fulness of the many aspects of the truth of revelation. The Roman Church strove to realize this fulness, but failed to appreciate the radical evangelical understanding of revelation. On the other hand, the Reformation saved evangelical truth at the expense of catholicity. A mutual process of correction and filling-out would be necessary if the Church were to grow to its true fulness. A concept similar to this is influential today in the German movement for Lutheran-Roman Catholic rapprochement known as "Die Sammlung", led by such writers as Hans Asmussen and W. Stählin.

The fundamental weakness in both Roman Catholic and Protestant work of this stripe perhaps lies in the use made of the concept of theological "values", or portions of the truth, which need to be joined together to constitute the Christian faith in its fulness. Although marking a significant step forward in Roman

Catholic attitudes towards non-Roman churches, Congar's schematism leaves no room for the conviction of Protestants that the theological "values" held by them, whatever they may be, are forms in which the *whole* Christ is present among His people: that they function as such in Word and Sacrament and are received as such by every believer. So long as the ecumenical question is visualized in terms of a jigsaw puzzle, to which different churches have differing contributions to make, the real nature of the problem of catholicity cannot be grasped. Congar, of course, makes no such mistake with regard to his own communion. But his view, by implication, forces others into this position, leaving them without any satisfactory starting-point for approaching the ecumenical task.

Of more direct influence on recent thinking within ecumenical organizations have been efforts to deal with the problem of catholicity in terms of church life in Great Britain. In 1945, the Archbishop of Canterbury invited Dom Gregory Dix to convene a group of Anglicans of the "catholic"[1] school of thought "to examine the causes of the deadlock which occurs in discussion between Catholics and Protestants and to consider whether any synthesis between Catholicism and Protestantism is possible". The report of this group was published in 1947 under the title *Catholicity: A Study in the Conflict of Christian Traditions in the West*. Similar invitations from the Archbishop went in 1947 to a group of Anglican "evangelicals", and to a group of British Free Churchmen. The reports of these groups were published in 1950 under the titles *The Fulness of Christ: The Church's Growth into Catholicity* and *The Catholicity of Protestantism*, respectively.

These reports form a single discussion which marks a considerable advance over previous work in that it takes the historical dimension of the subject seriously. The papers assume that there is a central thread of Christian tradition which constitutes what is given us by God, and they examine the way in which the

---

[1] Here, of course, "catholic" is not used as an adjective describing the Church as such, but as a designation of a particular school of thought within the Church.

different churches have, or have not, given expression to it. They also acknowledge that what is given us also sets a task before us. What is disappointing is the extent to which these three reports seek to justify the ecumenical centrality of the traditions they respectively represent. The Anglo-Catholic paper, which was published first, sets this tone, and the other two papers (especially the Free Church document) are in the nature of replies to it. On the Anglo-Catholic side there is so much misinformation concerning the Free Church tradition to be corrected that the Free Churchmen never really address themselves to their own tasks on their own lines. What is more, the impression is given that only the "catholic" party is really concerned about catholicity, while the "protestants" merely do their best to stay in the debate. This impression does not do justice to the real situation. But it is hardly fair to expect to find a distinctive "protestant" view of catholicity, if such exists, in a discussion whose terms of reference reflect mainly the internal problems of Anglicanism. In such a situation the "protestants" are certainly not silent. The real problem is that they react defensively and thus play false to their own best insights. The ecumenical movement, and eventually the entire Church, is then the loser.

Catholicity in the New Ecumenical Situation

Whatever may be the value of the studies just mentioned, it is clear that one cannot ask the question of catholicity in its contemporary form without probing deeply into the status of one's own church in ecumenical confrontation. This is what makes the concept of such great potential usefulness in examining the theological basis of ecumenical decision. If existing approaches to this question are not fully satisfactory, then more work needs to be done. For nothing is so important to the ecumenical movement as theological developments which take place *within* the various churches. These are the changes which will lead to an ecumenical revolution in depth. If the meaning of change is not understood by the churches concerned, ecumenical developments will take place irresponsibly or not at all.

It has already been suggested that much existing work on catholicity from the protestant side is unduly defensive in spirit. This is partly because the theological initiative to discuss catholicity, as well as much of the terminology employed, has so often come from "catholic" sources. But, more than this, the whole discussion has been carried on in the atmosphere of self-explanation, and even self-justification, which marked ecumenical conversation virtually up to the Lund Faith and Order Conference of 1952. The question of catholicity has not yet been properly raised in the context of developments since that time. Almost all the relevant literature on the subject in fact antedates Lund. Since 1952, there has been a shift of interest away from studies by churches of their own positions in the direction of common research on major topics of dispute. This in itself has occasioned new theological departures which now need to be carried back into the churches. Neither a simple self-justification nor a defensive attitude is now appropriate. Catholicity can now begin to be considered on a new basis.

What follows in these pages, therefore, is not intended to be another confessional or denominational apologia. It is an attempt, rather, to see catholicity in the light of the discovery of the Church by the churches, which, it has been claimed, is the new theological characteristic of our time. The intention is to ask what *this* situation means for the status of "protestant" churches, and for the decisions they must make.

The new situation that must be dealt with is at least partly represented by the great growth in importance of the World Council of Churches itself. The Church which the churches have discovered cannot, surely, be identified with the World Council; but it is within the fellowship of the Council that the discovery, in concrete terms, is very often made. Our new attempt to understand what catholicity means must therefore confront head-on the question of what the Council *is*. We must ask how it is relevant to speak of ecumenical decision-making by individual churches in the face of the conciliar relationships to which they are committed. The following chapter deals with this subject in detail.

2

THE CONCILIAR EXPERIMENT

THE FORMATION and growth of the World Council of Churches has injected a potent new factor into the ecumenical movement. It is important to notice just how new the *conciliar* expression of ecumenicity is. The ecumenical movement as such is generally dated back to the Edinburgh Missionary Conference of 1910. Identifiable ecumenical impulses, of course, can be discerned much earlier. But the World Council as such was only established in 1948. The significance of this fact, of course, is that the ecumenical movement has not *always* been organized in the conciliar form we take for granted today. Indeed, it might easily have been developed along some other line. When, in the 1930's, leaders such as William Temple, J. H. Oldham and others conceived the idea of a World *Council* of Churches, the proposal involved a tremendous risk. A council would make the ecumenical commitment of the churches to each other far more concrete and visible. It would bring tensions out into the open. It would test the strength of the churches' determination to stay together. On the ecumenical scene, the World Council was, and is, an adventurous experiment.

It is true, of course, that councils of churches on the local and national levels have existed for many years. But, despite surface similarities, these bodies have not, up to the present, represented quite the same reality as the world organization. The latter actually incorporated the movements of Faith and Order and Life and Work. It was not merely a co-operative agency for common pursuit of peripheral ecclesiastical concerns. From the beginning it crystallized in organized form all that was most significant in world ecumenical relationships. There was thus at the outset a difference in kind, as well as in scale, between the World Council and local councils. The World Council fell heir to more central Christian concerns. It was given the resources for greater theological responsibility. It has been used by the churches to speak for them and act for them in ways which local and national councils, with a few notable exceptions, have not yet attempted. The recent growth in significance of national and regional councils, indeed, has followed upon, and to some extent borrowed from, the example of the pioneering world organization.

Now the crucial question is this: Does the existence of the World Council of Churches place the question of catholicity in a new light? Have the churches created something more than a mere council? Something which in some way *embodies* their discovery of the one Church? If this is in any sense the case, our understanding of our own catholicity, and of the basis on which ecumenical decisions ought to be made, will undergo a profound change. In place of a situation which forces us to say that the Church cannot be divided and yet obviously is, we will have a situation in which certain signs of the one Church begin to appear tangibly among us. There will be areas of common action in which the antinomy is actually broken down. The appearance of even a rudimentary "churchly" reality going beyond and enveloping the boundaries of the existing churches ought significantly to alter the perspective of ecumenical discussion.

It is hardly possible, of course, to discuss whether the World Council has, or could have, such a status on the basis only of its constitution and official pronouncements. The documents insist, in effect, that the Council exists only to do the churches' bidding, and that membership in it need involve no change in the views held by any church about itself or about other ecclesiastical bodies. The Council is not a church itself, nor does it seek to prejudge the "ecclesiological question". It is neutral concerning the form which Church unity ought to take. These points are all made clear in the Toronto Statement of 1950 on *The Church, the*

Churches, and the World Council of Churches, a declaration re-affirmed as recently as the Third Assembly in 1961. Such official statements are necessary to reassure both present and prospective members of the Council that their convictions will not be compromised, and, moreover, that the Council is not and does not aspire to be a centralized power structure. Yet the reality that is coming into being may give the structure described by the Constitution a new meaning. Without in the slightest degree laying the Council open to the charge of becoming a "super-church", there may come deeper understanding and confidence between member churches, new ways of using the Council's facilities, new readiness to acknowledge the mind of the Church *in* the work of the Council: developments that may transform the conciliar relationship into a powerful "churchly" force in its own right.

The Scaffolding and the Skeleton

The theological issue involved here can be stated simply. What is the relation between the unity we have in the World Council and the unity of the Church of Jesus Christ? How far and in what way can the conciliar structure represent the latter unity, be an earnest of it, now or in the future? In recent years, discussion of this question has often taken the form of debate between proponents of an "organic" view of unity, and advocates of a "federal" view. The former standpoint has tended to consider councils, at most, as a kind of scaffolding within which the churches can come to realize their essential churchly oneness. The latter, of course, has tended to regard councils themselves as the core, the framework, or the skeleton of a growing together-ness between ecclesiastical organizations, and has taken this as the true ecumenical goal.

The most distinguished representatives of the two sides of this debate have perhaps been Bishop Lesslie Newbigin on the one hand, and President Henry P. Van Dusen on the other. It is important to note how these writers actually state their views, for in both cases the nuances of the argument are brought out in such a way as to save the discussion from false oversimplification. In his books *The Reunion of the Church* (1948, revised edition 1960) and *The Household of God* (1953), Bishop Newbigin suggests that councils are *a* form of our being-together in Christ, and indeed an indispensable form at the present time, but that they are not *the* form which the unity of the Church universal should take. Highly valuable as means to the ends which the ecumenical movement seeks, councils nevertheless become dangerous if they are mistaken for the goal of efforts to unite Christendom. The normative pattern of ecumenical progress, for Bishop Newbigin, lies in union negotiations between churches in each place, and therefore in an ever-expanding and ever more inclusive pattern of achieved churchly unity the world over. By contrast, in his *One Great Ground of Hope* (1960), President Van Dusen urges the churches to seek unity precisely by devolving more and more of their administrative functions on councils as such. He foresees a time in which church executives will make nearly all their important decisions in common with the executives of other churches in the conciliar relationship: when, indeed, virtually all activities of the churches will be conceived, launched, and administered by conciliar instrumentalities. Thus the unity that counts, a "functional unity", can grow and become effective.

Unquestionably, Bishop Newbigin's view has been the prevailing one within the WCC itself, and particularly within the Department of Faith and Order. It is most in harmony with the stipulations of the World Council Constitution. Furthermore, it is the only position that can now be officially taken if the Council wishes to continue relations with churches having highly "catholic" ecclesiologies. By contrast, Dr. Van Dusen's standpoint appears to reflect an ecclesiological position bound to the administrative, or functional, predilections of the churches of North America. Dr. Van Dusen, moreover, scarcely seems to regard actual unity negotiations between churches as worthy of mention. It could surely be said in reply that only if we are concerned to be one Church and to become such by organic union, can we expect to extricate the Body of Christ from bondage to large-scale organizational concepts borrowed from the business world. Only in Bishop Newbigin's view, it would seem at first, is there hope for a recovery of genuine churchliness.

Yet the time has come to ask whether the prevailing standpoint, for all its intrinsic importance, is adequate for the present ecumenical situation. Unity negotiations as such have become unexpectedly difficult. When the Church of South India was established in 1947, the World Council did not exist, much less such an organization as the East Asia Christian Council. The South India union was actually shaped on the basis of an optimism about the future of unity conversations elsewhere that has since been shown to have been problematic. May it not be time to seek ways in which councils can take a more active part in promoting unity? Can councils afford not to promote churchly unity as a theologically necessary accompaniment to their own organizational growth? If so, their ecclesiological significance will have to be thought through once again.

Moreover, is it not possible that what Dr. Van Dusen is saying goes a step beyond the old "federal unity" argument? At least potentially, his proposal involves something more than a purely federative concept of unity. If the churches poured more and more of their functions *as churches* into councils, the councils would take on increasingly churchly form. Might it not work out that such functions as confirmation, ordination, and the celebration of the sacraments could be increasingly exercised *within* the conciliar relationship? The result would be that in certain areas at least the councils functioned as churches themselves. This is not to say, of course, that it would be possible to persuade all the member churches of the World Council to hand over such functions without going through a theological process just as vigorous as that involved in the normal unity conversation. But here would be an alternative to the agonizingly slow growth of unity by repeated negotiation: church by church, country by country, region by region. There would be the possibility that unity might grow, instead, topic by topic, point by point. With such an outlook it would be possible not only to give immediate

relevance to Faith-and-Order conversations, but also to conse
the theological gains that are so often lost in the distances of t
and space that separate unity efforts from each other today.

If there is an element of unworkable speculation in what ha
just been said, it may none the less serve the purpose of showing
that it is no longer possible to rest content with the sharp alternative between the scaffolding concept of the Council, and the concept of the skeleton. Neither viewpoint, in its simple form, will
do. In fact, the alternative itself is misleading, for the Council,
without being either *a* church or *the* Church, is inextricably involved in the fate of the Church. The conciliar experiment, in
short, is something that neither can be nor ought to be kept
theologically neutral. And if not, it is of great importance that its
theological meaning be worked out openly and deliberately. It
will be maintained, indeed, in what follows that the *reality* of
World Council activity is already pressing the Council towards
some theological conclusions concerning its own nature which
must eventually be brought out explicitly.

The Significance of Ecumenical Theologizing

Possibly the most noteworthy fact about the actual operation
of the World Council is the quality of the theological insight its
activities seem to generate. The Council is a reflective body. Its
work has proved to be a constant source of exegetical, doctrinal
and practical thinking which the churches are able to share, from
the outset, in common. In the preceding chapter the suggestion
was made that the churches have not yet learned to take over this
material in ways that might lead them to change their actual
ecclesiological positions. But the very existence of such a growing body of insight is already a fact of ecclesiological importance.

The theological products and by-products of ecumenical
activity are so numerous that any detailed description of them
would be out of the question here. The material in question
comes not only from the Faith-and-Order Department, but from
all the activities grouped together under the Division of Studies
and beyond. This theological efflorescence itself demands an

explanation. The determination of Christians to think ecumenically has been an unexpected key to theological riches. No longer is it simply a question of accommodating conflicting confessional positions and church systems to each other. A whole new context of discussion is growing up, in the light of which encounter between churches will necessarily take a new form. Ecumenical studies themselves are necessarily geared to the requirements of available personnel, established programs, and projected meetings. But, taken together, they have an important common characteristic. They are concerned about what it *means* to be the Church in different practical situations, in different intellectual realms.

In consequence, of course, ecumenical studies differ both in subject-matter and in method from studies carried on in theological faculties. They are not concerned about historical and linguistic investigation for its own sake, nor are they usually involved with dogmatic questions as such. Ecumenical studies rather seek out what it means to say that all theological work is carried on in the Church and on behalf of the Church, "to discern the Body of Christ" in the *midst* of what goes by the name of theology. This is not simply a preoccupation with the "doctrine of the church" as such. It is the discovery of a perspective in which the whole realm of theological reflection takes on new significance.

This surely is the underlying motivation in the actual choice of research projects and techniques for the Council. The effort is always to embody the sense of the wholeness of the Christian faith even when specific topics hold the center of attention. For example, the "christological concentration" of the past decade has been far more than a comparative study of christological ideas. It has been a study whose presupposition is that the Christian faith *is* Christ, who lived, and died, and is Lord of His Church. This conviction, indeed, has been back of the renewing power the Council has felt in biblical theology as such. The effort here has not been simply to bring the various doctrines of the different churches to the bar of Scripture, for Scripture, as such, does not offer a basis of choice between competing doctrinal viewpoints. The thrust of biblical theology, rather, has been in the double conviction that Christ is the center of the Bible and that the Bible is the book of the whole Church.

Now it might appear, and has appeared to some, that the product of such insights will eventually be some unified "ecumenical theology". That is not the intention. It may well be that at any given moment some particular school of thought of confessional outlook will have great influence in some phase of ecumenical theological work. But all that has been said is, both in principle and in practice, compatible with a continuing theological pluralism. This fact, indeed, draws attention to an essential characteristic of ecumenical theologizing. It discerns the one Church in the multitude of theological expressions of the gospel, and, in turn, it situates these expressions within the one Church. This does not mean that the various theological positions remain unaffected. But they are certainly not replaced by any official theological line imposed from on high. They are merely placed in a catholic context. In so far as they bear a valid witness to the gospel, they are not asked to change into something else. Yet the process of ecumenical study does alter the terms of theological debate in a remarkable way. The theological issues which separate the churches do not become less important, but they lose their capacity to cause schism. It becomes clear that the theological controversies of the past no longer need be regarded as debates between rival claimants to God's exclusive favor, but as doctrinal debates *within* one indivisible Church.

Now an organization within whose fellowship such a theological discovery can take place cannot be considered entirely unchurchly itself. The point is not that the Council attains a teaching *magisterium* in its own right. It does not claim to teach true doctrine, or to exemplify proper church order. But it does have an inescapable concern for the integrity of the gospel in the Church, however the gospel is expressed. It has a concern that wherever the gospel is preached it shall be the gospel of the whole Church in all ages and times. In the present divided state of

Christendom, the Council not only provides an arena in which the catholic dimensions of Christian thought can emerge: it also shows the churches how they can give practical effect to these dimensions of the gospel in ecumenical witness, service and action. The many ideas generated in ecumenical encounter are thus more than isolated insights and random suggestions. They are instruments for communicating the discovery of catholicity which the churches have achieved through the Council and within it.

It is this fact, the writer thinks, that gives ecumenical pronouncements their true authority. Not all suggestions and proposals coming from Geneva are of equal value. Many are frankly experimental, tentative, and at times even mischievous. Not every piece of theological research done under ecumenical auspices is equal in quality to the best work available elsewhere. To speak of the "intrinsic merit" of ecumenical theologizing is perhaps to miss the greater point: that the Council is gradually moving towards a juncture at which its most representative and careful conclusions will have a claim to being taken as the mind of the Church. With increasing participation by Roman Catholic scholars in study activities, it may be possible soon to make this suggestion still more seriously. Then the question of the ecclesiological significance of the Council will have to be raised in some new way.

Toward an Ecumenical Church Discipline?

The crucial question, of course, is whether the growing, quasi-churchly authority of the World Council can be, or ought to be, acknowledged in any tangible way. Already there exist various limited forms of *de facto* recognition. On the one hand, the churches borrow theological ideas from the Council and take them, so to speak, into their own ecclesiastical systems. There is no question, for example, but that insights concerning the laity, youth, interchurch aid, world mission, and many other topics, have been developed in the Council and then adopted by the churches themselves. Sometimes the thinking in question has originated within a given church and then gained broader currency. Sometimes it has been hammered out at an ecumenical meeting or by the Council staff. The fact that an idea has come through ecumenical channels gives it a certain, not easily definable, status. But when the churches make such an idea their own, it becomes part of the Church as such. Likewise, the churches occasionally take actions implying an ecclesiastical recognition of the Council's activities. The most important example of this, of course, lies in the celebration of Holy Communion at ecumenical meetings. For such cases, at least one church modifies its rules concerning intercommunion and intercelebration in specific recognition of the fact that such meetings are held to promote the visible unity of the Church. Moreover, while the celebration remains under the authority of the church whose ministers officiate, it is normal for arrangements for such services to be made by the authorities of the Council itself.

These developments and their implications do not suggest that the Council is gradually moving into a position from which it could either make authoritative confessional pronouncements or authorized ministers preach and celebrate the sacraments. They do, however, suggest that the Council is already becoming *in some respects* a churchly body, and that the member churches implicitly wish it to be so. The churchly functions the Council now performs flow directly from the fact that it *is* the only visible, tangible place in which the catholic implications of its own theologizing can begin to be put into practice. Using the Council as an instrument, the churches can express the catholic character of their own existence in practical ways. Although there is no such thing as an ecumenical *ordo* or an ecumenical theology, there may thus be such a thing as an ecumenical *discipline*.

An ecumenical discipline, as the writer sees it, would emerge out of explicit acknowledgments by the churches of areas where they could extend their existing disciplines in order to be the Church together. Such a discipline would make use of conciliar facilities, but it would nonetheless be an expression of the life of the churches as such. Wherever possible, the actual structures of polity and canon law under which the churches now live would be broken down in specific ways so as to use councils in a genuinely churchly manner. This proposal, of course, would in no way reduce the pressure on the churches to seek organic union. But it would seek to distinguish between those elements of churchliness which might now be bodied forth in conciliar structures, and those elements which ought to be expressed in a unified way only with full-scale accord on the problems of ministry, the sacraments, and the nature of the gospel. It would recognize the conciliar relationship as a *churchly* earnest of the unity yet to be fully realized, without abandoning the goal of uniting Christendom, not in a council, but in one Church of Jesus Christ.

The possibility of working out such a concept of ecumenical discipline would depend in part on the theological recognition churches might be willing to accord to present ecumenical practices, and in part on the possibility of establishing a generally acceptable distinction, as well as relationship, between "discipline" and such realities as *ordo* and *confessio*. For most branches of Christendom, church discipline might be termed the practical expression of what *ordo* and *confessio* imply. Discipline would normally include such matters as rules for the practical life of ministers and people, regulations for the celebration and reception of the sacraments, definitions of various forms and degrees of ecclesiastical jurisdiction. Many a church would still maintain, of course, that its own particular discipline is the only valid reflection of its view of the gospel. But increasingly often it is realized that there is a dialectical relation between gospel and discipline which offers some help of flexibility. On the one hand, the gospel must always be expressed in *some* particular discipline. But on the other hand, the truths we confess and the ministry we share always say more than any singly disciplinary structure can body forth. We recognize in our understandings of *confessio* and *ordo* elements which tend to transcend our disciplines quite apart from ecumenical relationships. Now the value of organized ecumenical bodies may very well lie in the fact that here, at last, exist structures into which our disciplines can flow in an orderly way when they *are* transcended by new theological insights. It is no longer necessary to maintain a contradiction between our awareness of the necessity of discipline and the knowledge that our own particular discipline is not adequate for what we understand the gospel to be.

If such suggestions were to win acceptance, it might be possible to ask the churches to regularize certain kinds of ecumenical ministry that already exist. The churches could be asked to enact disciplinary ordinances that *included* duly sponsored ecumenical activities, and, in particular, ordinances enabling ecumenical agencies to begin to have a full life of worship, sacrament, and pastoral care. The authority of ecumenical agencies to provide such ministerial services might, of course, eventually be used to aid the actual extension of the Church to areas and situations that could not be treated as well by denominations acting on their own. At the same time, it would still be stressed that none of the great theological questions of *confessio* and *ordo* had been solved. The churches would still be free to maintain their regular disciplines for all ordinary church activities. It would be clear that these ecumenical extensions of discipline applied only to situations both carefully defined and carefully controlled by the churches themselves acting together in their commitment to each other to be the Church in word and deed.

The development of a conscious ecumenical discipline of this kind, of course, might well prove difficult. There would certainly be resistance from many sources on doctrinal and ecclesiological grounds, as well as the fear that what was called "ecumenical discipline" might in fact be only a euphemism for greater centralized control of Church life. But it should be said again and again that the World Council and other councils are *already* engaging in churchly activities without being free to acknowledge the fact. Barring unforeseen catastrophe, these organizations are going to grow. Would councils not actually become more pastoral in character and more open to theological correction if it were agreed that they are churchly and expected to behave as such? Such thinking might even impede the rampant proliferation of purely administrative bureaucracy in ecumenical organizations and promote the growth of a conviction among the churches that councils are not foreign bodies but actually a part of themselves.

Confrontation within "Koinonia"

It will be clear, of course, that none of this means that councils can simply *become* the one Church, or that their development can take the place of union negotiations between churches. The real import of what has been said is that the existence of councils, and particularly of the World Council, materially transforms inter-church *relationships*, and that this fact must be acknowledged in all future theological discussion. It ought no longer to be possible for any church to consider its own nature and status without awareness of the fact that in the Council it *already shares a churchly reality with other Christian bodies*. In some ways, this changes everything. The lines between the churches are no longer absolute. Orders and sacraments are no longer either exclusive or self-sufficient. But, most important of all, the historic debate between the Christian confessions now takes on an entirely new form. It can now be seen that this is a debate not between rival churches but *within one Church*. If this is taken seriously, it will lead us to give a different reading to the whole history of doctrinal controversy in the past, as well as to take a new view of the movement of doctrinal history into the future. The Council is merely one point at which the essential unity of Church history becomes visible. Our real task is to draw out the meaning of this unity over the entire range of the historical experience of the Body of Christ.

May it not be, then, that the real achievement of the World Council has not been to make interconfessional discussion unnecessary but for the first time to render such discussion potentially unitive, rather than divisive? The method of "comparative ecclesiology", characteristic of Faith-and-Order discussions before the Lund Conference of 1952, tended to force churches into the position of using self-explanation as a subtle means of self-justification. It has been possible to move beyond this position not only because of the particular theological method which the Lund Conference devised, but because of a growing conviction that the common ground among the churches itself has a churchly character. This has made it possible to regard both schisms and reunions as events *within* the Church. It has given real point to the aphorism of Nikos Nissiotis: "It is impossible to imagine any ecclesiastical event taking place *extra ecclesiam*."

Such a level of understanding had to emerge before genuine *theological* conversation between the churches could take place. For the questions that still need to be discussed between the great Christian confessions—Anglican, Reformed, Lutheran, Orthodox, Roman Catholic, Free Church—are churchly questions. They are not simply speculative, or sociological, or "religious" questions. They can be meaningfully posed only within a churchly context. If such a context exists and is acknowledged as such, the debate can go on: not in the interests of mutual accommodation at any price but in the interests of finding Christian truth.

The existence of the World Council is not in itself an answer to the question of catholicity. But it does enable us to ask that question in a new way. The question of what one's own church tradition means must now be asked in the churchly presence of all other Christian traditions. The question must be dealt with not in a purely independent investigation but as part of the ongoing theological work of the one Church. With this in mind we do not ask, self-consciously, what we might contribute to some future church union, or how the credentials of our tradition could be established in the eyes of others. Rather we ask what it *means* for the one Church of Jesus Christ that our tradition has in fact existed by God's grace within it. The subject of discussion *is* the Una Sancta, not merely our own particular part of it. The following chapter seeks to open up this question by looking at the subject in its historical dimension.

3

THE REFORMATION IN CATHOLIC
HISTORY

IF THERE is but one Church of Jesus Christ, this cannot be something new. What the churches have discovered in their conciliar relationship has been, in principle, an attribute of God's People in every age. It has been so as much in times of fragmentation as in periods of reunion. The wholeness, the catholicity, of the Church has been fundamental to its being even when that wholeness has been strenuously denied by outward events.

We should therefore be able to talk about something which might be termed *catholic history*: the history of the Una Sancta considered from its very beginning as one. We should be able to rethink the meaning of our common past in such a way as to make the unity of God's purpose within it emerge. The value of an effort to accomplish this could be very great. Each tradition, after all, is what it is because of its particular history. Yet each particular history participates in the one history we have together. If the meaning of catholicity could be discerned *within* history, in terms of actual historical facts, the present confrontation between traditions in the one Church might be seen in a new light.

This is the point, it would seem, at which a new approach to the problem of catholicity could well begin. The formulation of a concept of catholic history would be, in effect, an attempt to read the present ecumenical awareness not only into the problems the churches face now, but also into the whole substance of their past. In this way, ecumenical concern might do more than play across the surfaces of the different Christian traditions. It might go down *into* the historical dimensions in which they took form, rooting out obstacles to deep mutual understanding, and bringing to light mutualities that now lie hidden. A concept of catholic history, however formulated, would make it impossible to regard either events or ideas in the history of any given church as theologically self-subsistent. Without denying known facts about the past, or wishing to be dissociated from them, the different churches might come to see their own histories in a way that would release them from bondage to the letter, and free them to interpret them in the light of the total work of the Holy Spirit.

Catholic History and Historical Method

But such expectations will not be fulfilled without a careful attempt to define what catholic history is. The unity of the *whole* of church history is, in the first instance, a theological idea: not a visible empirical fact. How can such a concept actually influence the way history is read and understood? So long as it remains merely an idea, the answer is probably that it cannot do so to any great extent. But now, the catholicity of church history is becoming historically embodied. The conciliar relationship between the churches is beginning to bring this idea *into* history. From this toehold, it may be possible to work both forward and backward in history, and thus gain ground for the ecumenical movement that seemed irretrievably lost. The key to the whole thing is the embodiment of catholicity now. This is a reality of which historians as such must take account, and in the light of which all previous church history will look different.

But in what way, precisely, will it look different? In a general way, we know that it is possible for history to be "changed" by being seen from new vantage points. But at the same time, there must be some limit to the transformation history can undergo in this way, for the facts are still there. So far as Church history is concerned, misunderstanding, division, and conflict are facts which can be erased neither by theological ingenuity nor by subsequent ecumenical events. Hence the concept of catholic history forces us to be supremely realistic in ecumenical discussion. The wholeness of the Church is a reality which we can now see and feel, as well as think about, but the fact of division is also there and, historically speaking, it is beyond our power to change it or wholly to eliminate its influence upon us. How do these two realities interact in our actual study of the Christian past?

There are several levels of interaction to be pointed out, each of which makes some contribution to the reconstruction of history in catholic terms which we are seeking. The first level emerges among the most elementary fruits of the study of Church history *in common*. It lies in the simple recognition by historians of one tradition that they must take the histories of other traditions *into account* if they are doing Church history and not just sectarian history. This is hardly more than a raising of the problem, but it is of special importance in the historical discipline because of the unusual barriers that have separated church historians, as opposed, say, to biblical scholars, from each other along ecclesiastical lines. In so far as church history has been studied and taught within institutional structures, there has been a tendency to single out for special consideration the line of events that led to the emergence of the structures in question. Very often, too, there is methodological justification for doing this, because different church histories have in fact been largely institutionally distinct from each other, and thus actually capable of being dealt with as separate entities. But the ecumenical confrontation at least teaches the historian that he participates theologically in lines of history otherwise foreign to him, and that there is therefore pressure on him as a historian to see his material in the light of this fact. He will not forthwith discover some mystical harmony between events occurring at widely separated times and places, but he will very possibly ask questions of the data before him which he did not ask before. He will have the responsibility of trying to see other histories as *Church* history in the same sense as he sees his own, and of helping representatives of other traditions to see his own field of interest in that light.

A second level of interaction between catholic history and particular histories appears when historians of different traditions enter into dialogue about diverging interpretations of the same event or period. Here the focus is not upon the long stretches of separate history but upon the points of bifurcation. Where history-writing has been influenced by the attempt to justify past events in the light of divergent institutional consequences, there is bound to have been selectivity in the use of material that has blinded historians to certain relevant facts. There are a number of instances in which studies done in an ecumenical spirit have now produced more rounded views of certain germinal loci of Church history than were previously available. One such area is certainly the debate about the relation between Scripture and tradition in the Continental Reformation and Counter-Reformation. On both the Roman Catholic and the Protestant side, the nature of this struggle is being gradually clarified. Another flash of new insight, this time concerning the development of polity, has come with regard to the relations between the different Puritan factions in sixteenth- and seventeenth-century England. In most such cases it becomes evident that the actual event or period was not in fact quite what subsequent developments and assumptions could suggest. There is a recovery of definite, if limited, areas of catholic awareness which otherwise would have remained hidden within the historical documents. It is reasonable to expect this process to go much farther, especially in the realm of doctrinal debate: where all too often what was said even at the time *about* the views of the participants did not correspond with the actual facts.

But beyond this there is still another level at which the wholeness of Church history appears. When history is no longer seen merely as the multiplicity of outward events, but as the succession of the acts of God in Jesus Christ, the unity of the material becomes at least theologically evident. Is this unity manifest also in some tangible way? It can certainly be said that it has always been in some way manifest to those who *participated* in the historical events. The history of God's acts in His Church is the history of grace and judgement of the commending and condemning activity of the Holy Spirit. This is far from being an abstraction, for it is actually the very substance of the "Christian reality" historically considered. The closer one gets to the sacramental, devotional, or personal levels of history, the closer one is to what awareness there may have been of the catholic dimensions of Christian existence even in the midst of division. But how much of this is now available to the historian whose sources have been largely molded by the outward facts? It is simply not possible in most cases to "get inside" the records and documents to grasp the reality of grace and judgement they conceal. But it is not possible to examine Christian documents, on the other hand, without knowing that they would never have been produced at all otherwise. The reality of grace and judgement is thus implied not only by particular episodes of Church history but also by the very fact that such a thing as Church history exists. Moreover the history in which we grasp the catholic reality of God's action is the *same* history we examine critically, not a different stream of events utterly closed to critical investigation.

All three of these levels of interaction between catholic wholeness and empirical fragmentation in Church history are laid open for us by our study within the common ecumenical commitment. The "method" involved is nothing more or less than the determination to study within churchly fellowship and dialogue. Let it be stressed, however, that this effort is not to be equated with a simple attempt to write a "non-partisan" history of the Church. At the present moment, that would not be possible, and, moreover, it would not be useful. There is no question here of adjudicating past disputes, of deciding who was right and who was wrong. The purpose of such discussion is, rather, to trace the catholic reality we now know, back into our different histories in the confidence that this can illuminate the meaning of the paths we have travelled, and must still travel. The relation between the unity and diversity we discover in Church history resembles most of all the relation between unity and diversity we are finding in the modern study of the Bible. The historico-critical approach to the Bible is indispensable for gaining a clear view of the many diverse facts concerning the material with which we have to deal. But the unitive approach of "biblical theology" is equally indispensable for discovering what this material is really about. Moreover, biblical theology would be impossible without its historico-critical foundation, which already bespeaks the co-operation of a community of scholars committed to face the historical facts as they really are, knowing that the unity God has given to His People is given in and through real facts and not imaginary ones.

The Reformation: The Confessions and "Sola Scriptura"

What lines may be taken by historians of the Reformed churches who desire to see their own tradition in this catholic historical perspective? The first step, no doubt, is to see the material in its proper context within the general development of Christian thought and practice.

Originally, of course, the term "Reformed" applied to the whole Continental Reformation in both its Lutheran and Calvinistic branches. Our contemporary habit of employing the name only in connection with the Calvinistic churches and their descendants provides a useful terminological distinction but hardly does justice to the real situation. Lutherans have as good a claim to be called "Reformed" as Calvinists. It is theologically impossible in any case to treat Calvinism as a separate entity. The Reformation has significance in catholic history only if it can be considered as a whole, and it is our intention to do just this, if from a "Reformed" perspective, here.

It is easy to regard the Reformation as theologically a fresh beginning altogether, having little connection with the concerns of the fathers of Nicaea and Chalcedon. It is true that the distinctive themes of the Reformation make contact with New Testament language in a manner unrealized by the patristic writers, suggesting that the theology of the Reformers is basically a return to the faith of the primitive Church, standing in little or no continuity with any continuing, general development of Christian doctrine and tradition. It is often assumed, moreover, that this relationship of the Reformation to the Church of New Testament times provides the basis of the Reformation doctrine of theological discipline, *sola scriptura*. If the Reformers simply read off and reproduce the teaching of the Scriptures, they are immediately in possession of an apparently unchallengeable court of appeal on which to base the teaching authority of the Church. On this view, the Reformation becomes virtually a self-contained entity, and the question of its doctrinal relation to "non-evangelical" manifestations of the Christian faith is not seriously raised. Both the Lutheran and Reformed traditions, furthermore, are certainly distinctive in Christian history for having written numerous "confessions of faith" which purport to be summaries of the doctrinal teaching of Scripture. This proliferation of "confessional" writings in itself seems to underline the charge that the Reformation churches maintain an exclusive standard of orthodoxy, and indeed, that in their interpretation of *sola scriptura* they assume that the doctrine contained in the confessional statements is the only possible and completely sufficient reading of the biblical witness.

This rather dismal picture is deliberately chosen as a starting-point for several reasons. It is a position actually held in conservative theological circles, and it is a position not consciously denied by many who ought to know better. Furthermore, it is a viewpoint bequeathed to us by the tremendously influential period of Protestant Orthodoxy and enshrined in the constitutions of both Reformed and Lutheran churches today. There is no use painting an ecumenical picture of the Reformation without confronting head-on a view of the Reformation which is, in fact, constitutionally held by churches which trace their spiritual descent from it.

Two points, which have to do with the history and the intention of the Reformed confessions in particular, need to be made. The first is that the Church of Geneva in Calvin's time did not write a confession of faith at all. Strange as it may seem, therefore, "Calvinism" was not an "official" theological position of the Church within which Calvin taught. Reformed churches throughout Europe and America subsequently wrote "Calvinist" confessions for purposes which will presently be examined. But the mother Church of them all avoided taking such a position at the outset. This is important in that it shows, together with other well-known facts, that the fundamental intention of the Genevan reformers was to reconstitute the Church Catholic in that place, not to found a sect centered upon the doctrines of any particular school even if it was that of Calvin himself. It is significant, for example, that Calvin strongly opposed the promulgation of a "Protestant" confession of faith in France, the Confession of La Rochelle, because he feared it might obscure the equally catholic intentions of the French reformers. So long as there was a possibility that the whole Church of Jesus Christ in France might be reformed, Calvin believed that any formal proclamation of the theological position of the reformers themselves was bound to be divisive and self-defeating. As for Calvin himself, it is clear that he took his stand squarely *within* the ongoing history of Christian thought. One has only to note the frequency with which he refers, with positive appreciation, to the views of patristic and medieval writers: the *Institutes* are full of allusions to Irenaeus, Augustine, Bernard of Clairvaux, and Peter Lombard, to name only a few. There was no sectarian intention, much less a self-contained biblicism, at the origin of the Reformed tradition.

The second point, of course, is that when confessions of faith began to be adopted by the Reformed churches, they were written mainly for the purpose of supporting internal church discipline, and not for setting off the Reformed churches as distinct from others. There are very few cases in which it could be said that the Reformed confessions figured in debate concerning the churchliness of other bodies, or the relation of Reformed churches to them. It was assumed, following Calvin, that the Reformed position was theological discipline within, accompanied by ecumenical recognition without.[1] This interpretation finds support in the content of the confessions themselves. Adherence to the thought of the confessions is not among the *notae ecclesiae* that the confessions state. Word, Sacraments, and Discipline are the characteristic marks of the Church, and it follows that the Church must exist in all its fulness *before* it produces any form of written confession. Formal confession of the faith may be regarded as part of a given Church's fulfilment of the requirement of discipline, but it is not a basis on which one church can judge others. That another Christian body should take its theology seriously, and that its position should be a consequence of the faithful preaching of the Word, the Reformed churches characteristically expect. But that other churches should adopt the details of a particular Reformed confession has never been expected. This is the more obvious when one remembers how many different Reformed confessional documents there are, and how diverse are their theological emphases. A family resemblance exists among these documents, but no serious attempt has ever been made to unify them into one precise theological statement.[2]

What, then, *is* the rule of faith which brings the Reformed churches within the catholic tradition? The Reformed tradition does affirm the principle of *sola scriptura*, and it does set a high value on doctrine as such. But the whole history of the Reformed faith demands that these matters be seen in an ecumenical light. *Sola scriptura* operates within the Reformed tradition as a rule of faith, but this principle cannot for a moment imply that all our

[1] There was thus no counterpart among the Reformed churches to the extensive confessional debates within Lutheranism. The Lutheran confessions, for reasons that are obscure to the writer, have functioned *both* as internal disciplinary standards and as standards for external relations in a manner which makes the Lutheran confessional development quite different from the Reformed.

[2] An inquiry as to the possibility of such a unification of the Reformed confessional writings was made between 1880 and 1884 at the initiative of the great historian of dogmatics, Philip Schaff, but the difficulties appeared to be so great, and the possible advantages so slight, that the matter was not further pursued.

thinking is a simple transcription of the biblical message as it stands. Above all it cannot mean that Reformed doctrine has exclusive rights to be considered biblical. Rather, *sola scriptura* implies that the Bible must be continually alive and absolutely central within the thought and life of the Church, that it must be the source of new insights as well as the standard by which they are criticized. The church moves on in history and lives in many different cultural contexts and political situations. The proof of the validity of *sola scriptura* is not that the people of God are able to maintain a rigid, supposedly biblical, doctrinal position through every vicissitude, but that they find in every situation that the Bible does in fact speak to them, that it binds them to Christians of all times and places, and that it leads them to the new thinking which they must do if the Church is to maintain its witness and life.

The Reformation: The Ecclesiological and Soteriological Revolution

The upshot of this position is that one is free to consider the theology of the Reformers as in every way an open-handed contribution to the doctrinal history of the Church catholic, and, indeed, that one does not understand the Reformation properly *unless* it is seen in this light. Coming upon the Reformation in its setting in Church history, one is impressed that here two emphases, practical and theological, are intimately linked together. There is a tremendous emphasis on the recovery of the true face and form of the Church, a desire to discern the authentic body of Christ and to manifest it in the world. And there is the discovery of a new theological language in which to speak of man's relation to God in Jesus Christ: the language of grace, justification, and election. One sees the Reformation in its full significance only by grasping how the Reformers considered ecclesiology and soteriology to be related.

The familiar Reformation doctrines of justification by faith and election by God's free grace are, in the first instance, statements concerning the inner significance of man's adherence to Jesus Christ. But this does not mean that the Reformation introduced

c

an individualistic or pietistic emphasis into the gospel. It is true that both individualism and pietism followed upon the work of the Reformers as socio-religious phenomena, but it would be completely wrong to take the measure of Reformation doctrine in these terms. That such conclusions are sometimes drawn is only due to the fact that the Reformation is too often seen through the veil of our eighteenth- and nineteenth-century religio-romantic heritage. The Reformation may have opened doors through which certain forms of Christian romanticism walked, but the theological kernel of Reformation thought clearly lies elsewhere. The doctrines of justification and of God's gracious calling of men to His service are not psychological descriptions of the experience of evangelical conversion. They are disciplined attempts to work out the biblical basis on which a new humanity in Christ can exist in the actual conditions of human history. The fact that these doctrines spoke the language of men who were intensely and personally concerned with their own relations to God does not change their objective biblical character. Both Luther and Calvin, indeed, discovered the center of the gospel not in their respective experiences of doubt and striving, but in the conviction that God had already established the basis of new humanity *for them* by His deed of sending Jesus Christ in the flesh for all men. This was the discovery that a new manhood in Christ already existed in objective fact. Indeed it involved, by implication, a new awareness of the meaning of the humanity of Christ Himself: a humanity existing not only at a point of past history but a humanity presently real both before God in glory and in the empirical existence of the Church.

Seen in this perspective, Reformation soteriology can at once be translated into something approaching classical christological terms. The Reformation recovered a biblical sense of the manhood of Christ in history. It did not do this by a kind of Nestorian counter-emphasis to the somewhat docetic christology of St. Thomas and the medieval mystics. It did so by drawing out *in extenso* the affirmations already present in orthodox patristic christology, that Jesus Christ was fully and completely a man, and yet that His manhood can only be understood when we grasp that it was and is a universal manhood, for and on behalf of all men. In other words, the incarnation and atonement were not acts of God performed quite independently of man, but, on the contrary, God's work was carried on in the flesh of a particular man. Yet Christ's manhood had no *per se* existence apart from God's total drawing near to all of mankind, for the atonement was not simply a kind of individual human sacrifice, but a truly universal act.[1] Because God's work was inaugurated in *a* man, a historical person, the whole drama of salvation must be worked out in each generation in terms of actual human struggle. Yet because salvation is God's work, the man chosen by God must not assume that he is chosen on the basis of his personal merits, but because his election is a part of God's purpose for the *world*, and therefore a manifestation of free and prevenient grace.

The fact that Reformation soteriology can be translated into christological terms both demonstrates its essential continuity with the theological life of the historic Church *and* draws out the distinct contribution to the development of Christian thought which the Reformers made. Reaffirming the humanity of God in Jesus Christ, the Reformers restated the meaning of this humanity with a novel sensitivity to *historical*, and not merely metaphysical, issues. They tied christology in with the actual life of the Church in the world. It is through christology, indeed, that we see how Reformation soteriology and Reformation ecclesiology were linked. The real being of the Church *was* the new humanity in Christ, not the medieval institution with its hierarchy and canon law.

Thus, the ecclesiology of the Reformation was no more a theological creation *de novo* than was its soteriology. The christology of the patristic period was never properly brought to bear on the question of the actual life and structure of the Church.

---

[1] See on this point T. F. Torrance, "The Atonement and the Oneness of the Church", in The Scottish Journal of Theology, Vol. 7, No. 3, and reprinted in *Conflict and Agreement in the Church*, Vol. I, Lutterworth Press, London, 1959, pp. 238 ff.

Just as the medieval period philosophized the doctrine of grace, so it institutionalized the concept of the Church, to such a point that the prevailing understanding of the Body of Christ bore little real relation to the orthodox patristic doctrine of Christ's person. The Reformation, as Professor T. F. Torrance has shown,[1] sought to return ecclesiology to its proper christological setting. The very possibility of carrying out such a christological correction of ecclesiology, of course, depended on the fact that the Reformers had already developed christology considerably in a soteriological direction. Precisely by giving christological doctrine its proper dimension in continuing human history, the Reformers rendered it suitable for application to ecclesiological problems in a way that it had never been before. The upshot, of course, was that without denying that the Church *is* the body of Christ, the Reformers made it clear that it is so *only by grace through faith*. In this perspective, one can see how the Reformation took up the historic Christian orthodoxy and carried it forward to a new level of insight. The Church was indeed the body of Christ, but an institutionalism which failed to recognize that the being of the Church was *therefore* a matter of grace, and not of works, lost its hold on what the "body" really must mean in the actual, continuing life of man.

"*Ecclesia Semper Reformanda*"

The terms in which this has been put have been designed, hopefully, to make the point relevant not just for Reformation churches but for the whole Church. Whether it *can* in fact be understood or accepted outside the Reformation tradition is, of course, for those others to decide. At least there is material here for genuine dialogue.

The preceding pages have argued that the Church of Jesus Christ as such is subject to the principle of justification by grace through faith. Is this true? If so, what does it mean? The writer would contend that the meaning of this assertion is identical with

[1] "What is the Reformed Church?" in *Conflict and Agreement in the Church*, Vol. I, pp. 79 f.

the Reformation conviction that the Church is *semper reform-anda*. The reform of the Church is not simply innovation, and not simply response, however ingenious, to the challenges of the time. It is renewal of the Body of Christ by the grace of God received in faith. It is renewal which must go on all the time, and from which no aspect of the life of the Church is exempt.

It is no accident that we have recently been reminded of the relation between justification and the Church by Reformed theologians whose lives have been devoted to ecumenical renewal. Bishop Lesslie Newbigin, in the preface to the second edition of *The Reunion of the Church*, makes it clear that the whole theological movement towards unity is properly based on this principle.

> Is there, then, any other honest way of understanding theologically the issues involved in moving from disunity to unity? It is the main purpose of this book to argue that there is, and that the heart of it is to be found in the Christian doctrine of justification by faith.[1]

Professor T. F. Torrance has made a similar point in various writings. We are wrong to seek "justification" from each other in unity discussions, when the truth is that the Church stands or falls before God, who alone justifies.[2] Ecumenical relationships, involving as they do the shaking-up and renewal of the whole Church, certainly constitute a vital area for further reformation today. An understanding of justification in relation to the Church's life may well be the most important theological equipment which one can bring to the threshold of this ecumenical Reformation. Indeed, one may say more. If Bishop Newbigin and Professor Torrance are right about the ecumenical importance of justification, and if this chapter has thrown any light upon the theological basis of this principle as applied to the Church, the Reformation tradition may find a new and fulfilling

[1] p. xvi.

[2] See Professor T. F. Torrance's article in the *Bulletin* of the Department of Theology of the World Presbyterian Alliance, Vol. II, No. 1 (Summer 1961), pp. 6 f.

role to play in the catholic history of the twentieth century. It is all the more important, therefore, to add some comments about what the relation between justification and ecclesiology may actually involve.

The being of the Church rests upon the grace of God, and is justified only through faith in the redemptive historical work of God's Son. There are actually two ideas involved here. The life and form of the Church as such is *de fide*: that is, the structures and practices of the Church must stand in some analogy to the form of God's work in the incarnation. But the Church can only be the Church at all *per fidem*: that is, it is the grace of God, and not perfection of ecclesiastical form, which redeems the Church from being a congregation of disobedience. In other words, the visible structure of the Church is a matter of high theological importance, but yet no church structure can claim to guarantee that the Church so organized will be a true Church. These complementary principles are a direct reading of the implications of Reformation soteriology for the historical being of the new man in Christ, and thus deserve to be taken with ecumenical seriousness.

The form of the Church is *de fide*. This does not mean that man has faith *in* a particular structure of the Church as such, nor, on the other hand, that church structures are inconsequential so long as the Church lives in faith. The first tendency is that of Rome and Anglo-Catholicism; the second to some extent that of Lutheranism. That the form of the Church is *de fide* means that the government of the Church, as well as everything done by and within it, strives constantly to grow into mature conformity with the mind of Christ. It means that the visible configuration of the body of Christ should itself be a witness to Christ. Church doctrine and church discipline are thus inseparable. It is not possible, within a given ecclesiastical structure, to regard the way God's action in Jesus Christ is understood as indifferent to that structure, nor is it possible to apprehend our calling in Christ in a particular way and not make the structure of the Church a reflection of that apprehension. Christology and soteriology suffuse everything we believe about ministry and do about church government.

But this does not mean that the form of the Church must be rigid. The Genevan Reformation failed theologically at the point where Calvin and his followers attempted to deduce a particular blueprint of church government from the New Testament. Modern biblical and patristic scholarship has shown this to be an impossible task. But even without this, a literal transcription of Scriptural forms of Church life is not what making the form of the Church *de fide* means. What it means is that the Church should conform itself in the world to the true nature of the risen humanity of Christ in history. This may require radically different structures at different times and places. The New Testament offers many images which may be helpful in this task: above all, the image of the Servant of God as a kind of paradigm of the form of the incarnation. But more helpful yet, from a practical point of view, ought to be the theological flexibility which enables the Reformed tradition to see the moving *relations* between christology, soteriology, and ecclesiology. The bane of ecumenical discussion has been the tendency of participants to see only one way or another of relating these theological terms: to suppose for example that christology determines ecclesiology without any direct references to the doctrine of salvation (a failing which opens the door to the use of various philosophical or onto-logical schematisms not integral to the gospel), or to suppose that christology and soteriology are co-ordinate without any direct relation to ecclesiology (a failing which can lead to a kind of im-plicit docetism, or a lack of concern for the world). There ought to be a fulness and flexibility in the concept of the Church as existing *de fide* which could be brought out in an extremely creative manner from the ecumenical standpoint.

This, indeed, could only lead to a deeper grasp of why the very being of the Church is *per fidem*. However penetrating may be one's derivation of a particular ordering of the Church from the form of the humanity of Christ, the whole is worthless without an awareness that the Church is the Church only by the grace of

God. This is not simply a complicated way of saying that the Church will always contain an element of sin requiring forgiveness, but rather that to make the claim to be the Christian Church at all is sinful presumption except as we are continually taken up into God's purposes by grace received through faith. The Church can never be an object of faith, but itself lives only in faith.

This much said, it is perhaps possible to add a final theological point. It is hard to imagine how the principles of *de fide* and *per fidem* can be kept apart. If a church is serious about making its life and doctrine *de fide*, it will at once be evident that its being as a Church is *per fidem*, and that alone. If one begins with the principle of churchly existence *per fidem*, one will be inexorably led to seek to structure one's Church *de fide*. Is this not inevitably what the christology of the Reformation means when it is applied to the Church? Is it not necessary to avoid the formulations of particular philosophical schools on the one hand, and every form of dogmatic biblicism on the other, in order to get at the real being of the Church as the body of mankind redeemed in Christ, and understood by means of what Karl Barth has called an *analogia fidei*? That has been attempted here.

The ideal of the Reformation is *ecclesia semper reformanda*. The *ecclesia* here is the whole Church of Jesus Christ, not just the Reformed or Lutheran churches. It is important to take the implications of this seriously. In his book *The Coming Reformation* (1959), Geddes Macgregor points out that because the reforming movement failed to encompass all of Christendom, the churches that sprang from the Reformation were eventually satisfied with a partial apprehension of the fulness of catholic truth. They suffered particularly grievously in their concepts of liturgy and personal discipline. Dr. Macgregor registers an eloquent plea that the Reformed churches should recover this fulness themselves: that they should take unto themselves the full riches of Christendom and hold them *as reformed*, as if Christian truth had never been subject to the cheapening effects of schism. Certainly this would be to display the Reformation before the

Christian world not as a kind of secession from catholic history, but as a germinal event within it. Might this not, indeed, be the prelude to a new realization of our conviction that the Reformation must continue? It would certainly not be too much then to suggest that the other branches of Christendom should take unto themselves the riches of the Reformation and hold them *as catholic*. The unity of catholic history, which we know as a gift given us by God in Jesus Christ, would then begin to be manifest in terms that any bystander could clearly see.

4

REFORMATION, RENEWAL, AND THE SPIRIT

MEANWHILE, HOWEVER, there is a problem. It is all very well to talk about the Reformation in catholic history, but does the language we must use to discuss it actually *say* anything intelligible to the contemporary Church? Can the Reformation be brought up to date using sixteenth-century terminology, or is some kind of translation, or even transformation, necessary in our outlook if we are to appropriate the substance of what the Reformers were trying to say?

A very cogent argument could be mounted for the proposition that of all the theological positions in the history of Christian doctrine, the Reformed is the most difficult to maintain in the face of the conditions under which most of Christendom must now live. The achievement of the Reformation, as we have seen it, was to insist that the faith of the Church must be the ground of its visible life, and that the life of the Church must be lived in faith. As this actually worked out in the Calvinistic, or Reformed, branch of the Protestant movement, it meant a radical secularization of the Church. To read faith into Church life was to make Church life worldly. Not only were Christians to work out their vocations in everyday occupations, but the Church itself was to be a participating factor in society, rubbing shoulders in the market-place with the ideas and institutions of men. Yet, at the same time, the Church was to retain its transcendent basis. As a social institution, it was none the less to be the very embodiment of faith, the work of grace. It was to inject the actual substance of justification, or election, into human affairs: to be the meeting-place between the "new man" and the eternal God.

This picture is attractive, but does it mean anything today? Is it not true that this very interaction between the sacred and the secular in the Reformed understanding of the Church is what modern life forbids us to try to maintain? Are we not, rather, asked to choose between a socially irrelevant concentration on orthodox faith and worship and a socially useful accommodation to the *mores* and standards of contemporary culture? Are we not hiding the truth from ourselves if we insist that our historic position of tension can actually be lived out? Yet if it is not lived out, is there anything left of the Reformed position? It might well be possible to show that other Christian traditions have greater capacity than the Reformed to resist disintegration where theology and life in the world are forcibly separated. There are residual elements in both the "catholic" and "pietist" viewpoints which can and do carry on under conditions of great stress. Traditions of sacramental, liturgical discipline on the one hand, and concentration on the inner life on the other, both offer manoeuvring room for the Church when it is forced to the wall. But for the Reformed tradition there is no such possibility. Faith lives in worldly life, and worldly life lives in faith, or there is nothing. Here is both a weakness and a glory. A weakness, as anyone can see who discerns the frustrations and confusions of the typical, middle-class Protestant or Free Church congregation in the Western world. A glory, possibly, in the fact that if the disintegrating pressures of modern life touch the Reformed tradition so closely, there may be something in it of a sensitive nerve to warn the rest of Christendom of what its predicament really means.

The Divorce Between Faith and Life

Theology and life today tend to fly apart. It is necessary to look at the reasons for this more closely. Things have happened both to the life of the intellect and to life in society today which help to account for the problem; if these can be even summarily analysed, it may be possible to point a way forward.

In the first place, there is real doubt today whether "dogmatic" statements as such mean anything to most people, Christians included. Therefore it is all the more difficult even to conceive of making dogma the ground of our understanding of the Church. The Church at large has probably been protected from seeing the seriousness of this threat by the development of all kinds of pseudo-dogmatic theologies: dogmatics dressed up in the form of psychology, or of existentialist philosophy. But the fact remains that the theology of the Reformation was expressed in more or less literal statements concerning God's eternal nature, His purposes for man, and His actions in history, and we have reached a point at which the educated man has great difficulty in using such language either comfortably or intelligibly. How, one may ask, is it even possible to talk about grasping the essence of the teaching of the Reformation when this is our situation? But if dogma is dead, what is to be put in its place? Can the Church of the future exist without a vertebrate theology such as that expressed in our confessions and ancient creeds?

Here, despite the best efforts of theologians of every school, is a problem that remains unsolved. And in its wake has come another problem. The very meaning of embodying an articulate faith in the *form* of our church life has become foreign to us. The orthodoxy we have lost has been replaced by *orthopraxy*. Christian churches have borrowed power structures, administrative procedures, and patterns of parish life from organizations in the secular world. They have set up their own traditions of Christian reflection, because dogmatic theology cannot, seemingly, be made to apply to the problems we face. The Church becomes more and more a massive organization, sociologically linked with other such organizations, and almost on principle deaf to any protest founded upon the theologically informed conscience.

Some observers, of course, do not find these developments unpalatable. The death of dogma, they suggest, has come just in time to clear the way for Christian unity. And the rise of orthopraxy has, in fact, made Christian churches almost indistinguishable from each other already. But the ironic, yet undeniable, fact is that the liberation of Church life from dogmatic grounding has, so far, done little or nothing to make unity easier. On the contrary, the separation of Church practice from Christian doctrine in our day has left our structures and procedures without any chinks through which powerful theological solvents might be poured, any handles by which these customary forms of life might be seized and changed. This is not to say that we desist from trying to find theological rationalizations for things as they are in the Church. But our rationalizations neither recover nor replace the unity of doctrine and Christian comportment that was the heart of the Reformation faith. The separation we suffer between doctrine and life, indeed, is more serious and fundamental than the separation between church and church. It is the fundamental reason for our divisions. These divisions will not be overcome except perhaps in some superficial way, unless new life is discovered in Christian doctrine, and doctrine again becomes part of daily living.

The reasons for our predicament are not easy to diagnose. Any attempt to trace the whole difficulty to some single, well-defined source would certainly be rash. Yet certain factors in the situation are worth pointing out for the light they throw on our ecumenical tasks. At the time of the Reformation, it was assumed without much question that the whole creation could be understood in explicitly Christian terms. It was taken for granted, that is, that the world presupposed by the language of dogmatic theology was the same as the world studied by science, or the world in which men earned their livings. Theology did not occupy a compartment of its own, but was assumed to consist of statements about God, *and* about a world which anyone could see and touch. Thus it was possible to think of a unity between doctrine and life. It was possible to suppose that the structure and the government of the Church in the midst of the social order spoke relevant theological truths to man in society, and, conversely, that man's comportment in society could be directly interpreted in theological or ecclesiastical terms. Even if the relationship between theology and society was at certain moments negative, or even antagonistic, it was assumed that a relationship existed between them, and that debate could be carried on within a generally acceptable universe of discourse. At one and the same time the Church could be part of the human community and in touch with divine realities.

Now such assumptions were possible not because the being of the Church as such, somehow standing between Christ and culture and comprehending both, had been exhaustively explored. They were possible because men shared a common set of background assumptions within which all discourse, whether theological or sociological, was set. The *respublica christiana* was an affair of the intellect as well as of material civilization. The possibility of relating dogmatic truth to common life depended virtually entirely on the existence of uncriticized assumptions concerning the unity of human experience within a "Christian" culture. The minute such assumptions began to be questioned, the relations between dogma and life also began to appear problematic. The Church was forced to improvise oversimplified syntheses between doctrine and existence merely, so to speak, to keep body and soul together. Among such improvisations one could list many forms of pietism, many strands of the nineteenth-century ecclesiastico-liturgical revival, and virtually the whole "fundamentalist" movement. The basic fact, which none of these movements could change, was that the commonly accepted universe of *meaning*, within which Christian theology and human life had formerly dwelt together, no longer existed.

Today, of course, we live in a world in which this disintegrating process has gone to great lengths. It is still possible for Christians to *impose* comfortable patterns of meaning on the world about them, but the world has meanwhile found a language of its own: a language independent of theological presuppositions. The world talks back to the theologian. It resists his attempt to speak for it, or to tell it what it should be thinking. There is little echo of the theologian's language in the vocabularies of modern economics, politics, or technology. If there is to be any unity of faith and life for the Christian in the twentieth century, that unity must be generated from *within* a renewed Christian community, as a direct implication of a new understanding of the gospel. The Church, in short, can no longer borrow its wholeness from the world around it: *it must bring that wholeness into being itself.*

Here, obviously, we meet the question of catholicity in a new form. Gone is the time when a majority church, a "national" church, or a predominant church can assume its catholic status just because it apparently blankets the culture of which it is a part. There are, of course, churches which behave as if the *respublica christiana* still existed, still counting on their cultural surroundings to complete the wholeness of faith and life which they are unable to realize out of the Christian community as such. It can only be said that such churches are victims of an increasingly dangerous illusion. In them, just as much as in churches which frankly face the pluralism of modern culture, doctrine has lost distinctive meaning and the Christian life has become indistinguishable from the life of the ordinary pagan citizens. What is required is radical rediscovery of what Christian community *itself* means: a rediscovery, precisely, of the meaning of catholicity in its qualitative, not merely its quantitative, aspects.

Reintegration Through Biblical Renewal

Theologically, our hope that this may be done now rests squarely on the new attitude Christendom now takes towards the Bible and towards biblical theology. The power of renewal in the Church has been felt again and again where the Bible has spoken to groups of Christians gathered together in openness and expectation. The meaning of the Bible has been providentially reopened for us at the very moment when the medieval and Reformation syntheses between doctrine and life are in their final disarray, offering the Church the opportunity to recover its own distinctive being and message.

This, of course, breathes the spirit of the Reformation. It is supremely hopeful, but also extremely hazardous. Can biblical theology *really* do what is now being claimed for it in the ecumenical movement, and, if so, what are the doctrinal implications? It is important, in the first place, to see the contemporary biblical revival in the context of the disjunction between doctrine and life just described. For the ecumenical significance of biblical theology is not merely that it offers a way of getting behind dogmatic differences. Much more important is the fact that we think we see in our new approach to the Bible a way of re-forming the Church, as it were, from the ground up, to live under the new conditions which God has imposed on it.

The literature on this subject, of course, is vast. But it is not difficult to point to what is at stake both from the doctrinal and the practical points of view. The rediscovery of the Bible in our day has two main foci. In the first place, students of the Scriptures have recovered what has been called the distinctive "biblical point of viewing". They have entered into "the strange new world of the Bible" and mapped something of its structure and its presuppositions. This scholarly achievement has involved a variety of approaches to the material. It rests, in part, upon the results of literary and historical research, but it is also based on an awareness of the limitations of critical methods of study for grasping the thought of the Bible from the inside. The recovery of the biblical point of view has been facilitated by studies of Israel and the early Church both within their shifting intellectual environments and in contrast to them. Indispensable to the whole movement has been a growing sense of the unity of the biblical outlook, a common universe of presuppositions and attitudes which the biblical writers have in common despite the rich variety of their vocabularies and particular concerns.

But it is possible fully to understand this first focus of biblical theology only in the light of the second: the attempt to account for the Bible's surprising capacity to speak with arresting power in certain contemporary situations. The scholar becomes aware of the "strange new world of the Bible" at least in part because he knows that it is possible to enter into this world in a meaningful way today. It is not that groups of Christians shut their eyes, swallow hard, and make up their minds to think in terms, say, of a first-century world view. The point is, rather, that Christians discover that it is possible to stand in the same "place" as the prophets and apostles *before God*. The biblical point of viewing is actually viable in the twentieth century, and, under the right conditions, can be translated into twentieth-century terms at least so far as personal and communal commitment is concerned. When read inside the committed community, the Bible yields up its riches, and this, in turn, unquestionably indicates something about what the Bible essentially is.

But these two foci of Biblical study involve a sort of hidden dogmatic premise, and it is the validity of *this* which will determine whether we are on the threshold of a new understanding of Christian faith capable of drawing belief and action together again. The dogmatic premise of biblical theology is that we still live today within biblical history, within biblical time. In discovering the power of the Bible we are not discovering a universal human possibility of which the Bible and our particular experience are two salient examples. We are saying something quite different: that the providential action of God within history, to which the biblical writers bear witness, has continued from that day to ours, and that we live within that same historical continuity. Biblical history, in short, has not ended. We are still a part of it. In some sense, the actions of God towards men did not cease with the close of the canon, but continue in the life of the Church. Only on this presupposition, it must be stressed, can we really say that *our* experience with the Bible unlocks the inner meaning of the biblical world itself, for the Bible sets God's actions in a definite historical progression. If we are not within that progression, we cannot understand what the Bible is saying.

But this raises the whole question of the meaning of history. What do we mean when we say that God acts in history? In order to say any such thing it is necessary not only to say that God acted in the events of the Bible and that He acts in our lives but also that He has acted in intervening historical events which are neither biblical, nor, so far as we are concerned, personal. It is impossible, in other words, to escape into subjectivity. The whole enterprise of biblical theology rests on the premise that it is meaningful to say that God continues to act in objective historical events: events that can presumably be named and described by the historian, or the sociologist, or the journalist. Here, the writer must confess, he finds the present theological position unsatisfactory. The concept of *Heilsgeschichte* in all its varieties, the idea that there is a line of "salvation history" above, alongside, and within "ordinary" history, appears to leave us with an impossible gap between what the biblical theologian means by "history", and what historians mean by it. Likewise the attempt to recover the substance of biblical history by the use of existentialist categories of explanation is surely a retreat from the fact that the real history has its objective, as well as its subjective, side. Does it mean anything at all, then, to say that God works in history? If so, exactly what?

The question just raised is a theological question: a question, if the reader likes, that belongs to *systematic theology*. One cannot help feeling that so long as the biblical theologian is content simply to equate Christian theology with biblical interpretation, his work will fail to meet the real demands of the intellectual situation in which the Church stands. The point is often enough made that one finds theological meaning in the Bible only if one brings theological perspective to the study of the Bible. But now we are in a position to say something more. The study of the Bible today is *itself* demanding a new theological departure which will not be identical with any perspective we might have brought to the work at the outset. This is as it should be. It is what happened at the Reformation. What is needed now is the courage to grasp the dogmatic step which biblical theology requires us to make.

Let us be sure that the issue is posed in the right way. Throughout the course of Christian thought the fundamental problem has always been to do justice to God's presence in the world *in His*

very being. The great heresies—Arianism, Nestorianism, docetism—have almost always been forms of the denial of God's *real
presence* in and through Jesus Christ. The discussion, under-
standably, has taken different forms, depending on the particular
issues at stake at different times. Professor T. F. Torrance, for
example, has suggested that the issue in the fourth and fifth
centuries centered on the question of *revelation*. The fact that God
Himself meets us in Jesus Christ was important then because this
fact overturned all gnōsis, all unscriptural speculation, and
secured the truth that we know God only through God's own
work. At the time of the Reformation, clearly, the issue centered
on the question of *grace*. To say that God *Himself* meets us in His
act of grace was important in the sixteenth century because it
made clear that grace could be vouchsafed only by the Giver, and
through the sacraments of the Church only through utter de-
pendence on God's free act. Now the question of *history* with
which we struggle today is not essentially different. It merely
draws our attention to another set of relationships in which we
must try to understand what God's real presence in the world
means. The Bible demands that we try to understand *this*, just as
it prodded Christians of other times to try to comprehend other
aspects of the gospel. We must do justice to the Incarnation of
God in Jesus Christ in the new realm of discourse opened up for
us by our contemporary predicament, the realm of *world history*,
the arena in which mankind is finding a new intellectual auto-
nomy and a new, if precarious, life.

The Question of the Holy Spirit

The Bible, of course, does not leave us without guidance about
where to begin. The answer the Scriptures give to the dogmatic
question they themselves pose is that God is present in history by
and in His holy Spirit. The doctrine of the Spirit is implicit in
the *use* of the Bible made in modern biblical theology, and it is
implicit in the rediscovery of the *world* of the Bible that has gone
with it. We are not, of course, permitted to regard the Bible
exclusively as a treatise on the Spirit and thereby to ignore the

incarnation. But the specific way in which we must *read, understand* and *apply* the Bible today brings the doctrine of the Spirit to special prominence. The Spirit is the Bible's answer to the problem of God's real presence throughout the length and breadth of human affairs, building up man's institutions and tearing them down, speaking through prophetic utterance, illuminating the meaning of events. The Spirit is the form of God's presence we must grasp if we wish to substantiate the presupposition that we live right now in biblical time, and that the biblical point of viewing can be ours.

But we are certainly ill-equipped doctrinally to do justice to this question. Pneumatology has always been an area of confusion in Christian thought, and, indeed, it may not be unfair to say that at this point the ground-plan of doctrine is still incomplete. The Creed produced at the Council of Nicaea in 325 contained only the most perfunctory reference to the Spirit. When the Fathers at Constantinople in 381 expanded this third article of the Creed, they were able only to produce a result which George Hendry has described as "singularly meager . . . even . . . slipshod."[1] Hendry points out that this article not only omits explicit reference to the relation between the Spirit and the incarnate Christ, but also to the relation between the Spirit and the Church. Little has been done since 381 to formulate a doctrine of the Spirit which commands the universal assent within Christendom accorded the first two articles of the Creed, and the subsequent Chalcedonian definition. It is a striking fact, for example, that the Westminster Confession of Faith was originally produced without any article dealing directly with the Holy Spirit at all.

The result is that in reading what the Bible says about the Spirit we are blind and deaf. Centuries of doctrinal confusion, of half-truths, of fanatic enthusiasm, of institutional indifference, all weigh on our understanding and make it virtually impossible for the Bible to speak to us authentically at this point. It is not

[1] *The Holy Spirit in Christian Theology*, The Westminster Press, Philadelphia, 1956, p. 13.

merely that the doctrine of the Spirit is controversial. It is that it is in a state of captivity to the myriad ways in which it has been only partially apprehended, or even totally misunderstood. The first step, of course, is to be aware of our various forms of bias, particularly the institutional forms. For, ironically, it is the Church, which lives by the power of the Spirit, which has done most to imprison and distort our understanding of the Spirit's work. This can be documented with several examples of the positions actually taken by various churches at the present time.

The Roman Catholic position has been authoritatively summed up in the formula: "The Holy Spirit is the soul of the Church."[1] The presence and power of the Spirit are regarded by the Roman Church as endowments bequeathed by Christ to enable the Church to discharge her supernatural role. Hence the Holy Spirit empowers the Church to continue the mission of Christ in the world. The power and authority which derive from the Holy Spirit are held to be given to the Church herself to exercise: hence the Spirit is looked upon as a power active in and through the Church, but never over against the Church or in judgement upon it. It follows that there is a tendency in Roman Catholicism to think of the role of the Spirit as not personal but instrumental. Roman Catholic dogmaticians feel they must establish a *continuity* between Christ and the Church. Once this is done, there is no need to establish Christ's Lordship *over* the Church; for the Church already possesses the authority of Christ. Although, in theory, the Spirit is believed to be active in all the members of the body, the close connection in Roman thought between Spirit and ecclesiastical authority inevitably leads to an assumption in practice that those who *exercise* authority in the Church are more fully channels of the Spirit's action than others. If this is in any sense correct (so brief a treatment, of course, can hardly be adequate to the subject), it would seem obvious that the Roman Catholic understanding of the Spirit has been constructed to fit the Roman Catholic ecclesiology, rather than the

[1] A formula promulgated by Leo XIII in *Divinum illud*, June 20, 1896, and reaffirmed by Pius XII in *Mystici corporis*, June 29, 1943.

reverse. More important, the Roman Catholic doctrine of the Spirit reveals the Roman Catholic style of life. It indicates that the very principle of movement and renewal in the history of God's people is misunderstood. Far more serious than any given heresy or inadequacy in a Church is a viewpoint which cuts that Church off from genuine possibility of change by the grace and power of God. There is little value either in comparative ecclesiology or common ecumenical research if a Church does not know, theologically, what it means to move.

It might be supposed that an understanding of renewal by the Spirit would be the *forte* of that ecclesiology which stands at the opposite extreme from that of Rome. "Enthusiasm" exalts the sovereign freedom of the Spirit, but in such a way as virtually to sever the connection between the mission of the Spirit and the historical Christ. Here the emphasis is laid on the immediate, subjective experience of the Spirit in the individual. The attitude of enthusiasm would appear to be that the dispensation of the Spirit has *superseded* the historical revelation of Christ. Thus the purpose of the *filioque* clause in the Creed is left unfulfilled, and enthusiasm leaves itself with no objective criterion by which to "test the spirits". The irony of this theological position is that, informed by it, the Church moves no more decisively than it does on the basis of the outlook of Catholicism. Purely subjective experience is almost invariably conservative. Many contending opinions, each dignified by belief in the "right of private judgement", add up to no real renewal and no real action. Here, too, ecumenical research falls on deaf ears, for the Church does not know, theologically, what it means to move.

It is doubtful, furthermore, whether the main-line denominations of evangelical protestantism, including those of the Reformed tradition, can be given better marks. Protestantism has sought to maintain a balanced doctrine of the Spirit, but in all too many cases there has been a fixation on the issue of the "inspiration" of the Scriptures, as if the only function of the Spirit had been to guide the writers of Scripture in their composition and the readers of Scripture in their understanding. Not that this understanding of the Spirit is untrue so far as it goes, but the tendency to think of the Spirit only in connection with the words of the Bible is itself unbiblical. The Spirit is no more a guarantee of the inerrant transmission or exegesis of the words of Scripture than it is of the authority of ecclesiastical hierarchies or the reliability of our inward "spiritual" assurances. It is true, of course, that by relating Spirit to Scripture one stresses the doctrinal point that the Holy Spirit is the Spirit of Christ, but the *manner* in which this has been done in protestantism has worked a distortion of the doctrine. The work of the Holy Spirit in creation has been reduced to the banal concept of words inspired *in abstracto*. The result has been protestant legalism, which is, in essence, a lack of imagination about how and where, by the power of the Spirit, the words of Scripture come alive.

These remarks draw attention to a fact of major significance. Our doctrines of the Spirit are strongly conditioned by our ecclesiologies, and by the way we make our decisions and do our business as churches. It is probably true, indeed, that the doctrine of the Holy Spirit has been subject to such influences more than any other area of the faith. Officially, at least, we are astonishingly orthodox in our christological and trinitarian thought, and what is more, we tend to recognize each other as orthodox in such areas. But there *is* no standard of orthodoxy with respect to the person and work of the Third Person of the Trinity, and the implicit or explicit views we hold about the Spirit come straight out of our particular experiences as Churches, whatever these may be. If the Spirit is the key to understanding how God is present in history, then it is urgent for us to free this doctrine from imprisonment within ecclesiastical structures and presuppositions. The Spirit, according to the Bible, brings the Church into being. The Church does not in any sense create or control the Spirit. How can we do real justice to this truth in our day?

The Spirit, the New Creation, and the Church

The first step, without question, is to try to listen anew to what the Bible tells us the Holy Spirit *is*. A biblically grounded approach will permit us neither to isolate the Spirit from the rest of Christian doctrine, nor to domesticate it within any particular ecclesiology. Rather it will show us that when we speak of the Spirit we mean the moving, energizing work of the whole Trinity in the world: precisely the active presence of God Himself in creation. It is not, of course, as if the Spirit were the *only* mode of God's intervention in the created universe. It is rather that, when we speak of the Spirit, we see God's active presence from a particular standpoint: the standpoint of His continuing providence in and concern for unfolding events. If Christ is the *meaning* of history, then the Spirit is the *mover* and *maker* of history: yet not in such a way as to be independent of the incarnation, but, on the contrary, in such a way that the incarnation alone enables us to grasp the nature and significance of the Spirit's relation to constantly changing historical circumstances.

This can be put more precisely. Even with respect to Jesus Christ in the period of His earthly life, the New Testament assigns a large role to the Spirit. Christ reveals and proclaims God's will, but the Spirit is the power behind the mighty events in which He is the central figure. Jesus is conceived by the power of the Spirit (Matthew 1: 20), inaugurated in His ministry through baptism in the Spirit (Matthew 3: 16 and parallels), and raised from the dead by the Spirit (Romans 1: 4). The Spirit is that continuing mode of God's working in the world in relation to which the specific events of the incarnation take place. Similarly, God's People, both before and after the incarnation, are explicitly related to Christ by the power of the same Spirit. The Spirit speaks to Israel through the prophets (I Peter 1: 11), and subsequently creates and guides the Church (Acts 2; 15: 28; 16: 7). By no means is the Spirit said to be responsible for every revelatory event in the Bible, but it is clearly the uninterrupted presence of God in human affairs through His Spirit which makes it possible for Christians in every age to *participate* in biblical events with insight and power.

Now, fascinatingly enough, this biblical picture brings the *world* decisively back into our understanding of the gospel: not as a cultural matrix which we can simply assume to be "Christian", but as an arena in which God's ongoing work makes it possible for the Church to emerge anew wherever the gospel is preached. Biblical theology *assumes* that this is a world in which response to God's Word is possible. The biblical teaching about the Spirit urges us to venture boldly in trying to understand *why* it is possible. Christians must on no account retreat into a ghetto to escape a world which no longer speaks the Christian language. On the contrary, they must find new language to interpret the world creatively as the dwelling-place of God in Jesus Christ, living and acting by the power of the Spirit: the beloved universe where, when the Word is preached, new life can spring forth like water out of parched ground.

But what, then, are we saying? What can the Christian see in the world which the non-Christian cannot? Unquestionably, the biblical answer is that the Christian can see, interpret, and participate in the reality of *palingenesia*, "new birth", or "new creation". Repeatedly in the Bible, the work of the Spirit is intimately related with the appearance of new and shattering facts in the midst of the human environment: with the renewal of creation itself. The whole creation was, and is, involved in the incarnation, and nothing less than this is involved when the Bible speaks renewingly to us. It is not easy to grasp all that this means, but we cannot restrict the fact of renewal either to a purely personal context or to a purely ecclesiastical one and hope to understand it in its fulness. If we are renewed by the Spirit of Jesus Christ, we are taken up into the cosmic work of renewal being carried on by God. God's constant work of renewal is an existing reality, which we discern and thankfully acknowledge. It is the ground on which our own being as Christians rests.

Our awareness of all this cannot be translated into scientific historiography or cosmology, *and yet it does not allow us to leave the world alone*. We see the world in new dimensions which are more comprehensive than the secular dimensions of "nature", "history" and "culture". The New Testament treats renewal in terms of new relationships between redeemed man and the world of which he is a part: relationships for which there is no room in current scientific categories, but which yet unmistakably reveal otherwise unimagined aspects of reality. First among these is certainly the *discernment* of God's emerging purposes: above all in the midst of apparent chaos (e.g. Gen. 1:2; Mark 13; 2 Cor. 3). Life in the Spirit enables the Christian man not to be demoralized by chaos, because his life is not simply dependent on social or other structures that are constantly passing out of existence. On the contrary, it enables him to be sensitive to the new orders that are coming into being, to overcome his blindness, to speak out, to be free for action. Then there is the equally unexpected possibility of *intercession*, in which the Spirit teaches the redeemed man how to take on himself the groaning and travail of humanly distorted creation and to bring it before God (Romans 8). In intercession, we are given a double gift of the Spirit: the ability to identify ourselves with chaos (while the "natural" man perpetuates it by supposing that he, as an individual, stands apart) and the ability to carry chaos unchanged and unvarnished before the throne of God because we know what healing and forgiveness mean. And finally there is the possibility of *obedience*, in which we ally ourselves with God's purposes for the world and thus gain a sense that we are truly at home in creation (1 Cor. 3). This is in marked contrast to the estrangement from the world paradoxically felt by the so-called "natural" man, who is natural only to the extent that he is one of the majority of human beings who fight against their humanness, refracting God's purposes out of shape and proportion and turning creation into hell.

The theological task of thinking out the meaning of the Spirit's renewing power in creation is, of course, only beginning. The terms of reference just suggested may not turn out to be at all adequate. But if the *direction* is right, there may be enough here to show us where we are headed. The Church can no longer make the Christian faith relevant to human concerns by dominating the culture in which it lives, or by imposing its own interpretation upon culture. The Church can be relevant only by serving the Spirit of God in Jesus Christ which is already working creatively in the world. By sensitivity to the Spirit in the midst of human chaos, God's People can become the first-fruits of the new creation, the *palingenesia*. In discernment, intercession, and obedience, the Church not only can become aware of the Spirit, but can become a participant in what the Spirit is doing. There are two movements here. It is the work of the Spirit to empower the Church to suffer with the *whole* of creation in the particular kinds of groaning and travailing, building up and breaking down, characteristic of any given age. The Church is given by the Spirit to understand *how* mankind suffers, to grasp the exact shape of his agony, to articulate what he cannot articulate, and to turn it into prayer. But in doing this, the Church becomes precisely the point at which the new work of the Spirit becomes visible and tangible. For to undertake Godly obedience within creation and to intercede for creation before God is to participate in the continuing work of renewal inaugurated in Jesus Christ, whose Spirit is abroad in the created order.

Now there are theological possibilities here of potentially great ecumenical importance. A pneumatology freed from the ecclesiastical fetters in which it has been bound may well prove to be a matrix within which opposing doctrinal formulations can find a higher unity. Specifically, the "catholic" and "protestant" views of the Church, the ministry, and the sacraments may well seem less mutually exclusive if they are filled out in the light of the biblical teaching about the Spirit. We have debated endlessly the relationship between the ordinances of the Church and the gift of grace, overlooking the fact that there is far more New Testament material relating God's People and their *charismata* to the Holy Spirit than to "grace" as such. The sacraments, indeed, have nothing specifically to do with *charis* in New Testament thought at all. Both "catholic" and "protestant" theologians have too often limited their debate to personalist terms, forgetting that the real ecclesiological question has to do with the objective contemporary *being* of God in space and time. Our whole discussion of the Reformation in catholic history has been subject to this limitation out of fidelity to the sources, but now we must take a step beyond the traditional language in the knowledge that this language is no longer enough.

When we move the ecclesiological debate into the realm of pneumatology, the whole landscape changes. We are now dealing with our relation to God Himself: in His present, temporal existence. We cannot control God's existence in space and time to suit ourselves. Hence we uphold the Reformation protest that God gives Himself to men in gracious freedom, and not exclusively through the ministrations of any ecclesiastical body. But at the same time we affirm that what God gives us through His Spirit is *Himself*, and nothing less. Our relationship to God in Church and sacrament is not simply occasional and not simply forensic. Because God is truly present, that relationship is substantial and real. Transferring the discussion to the realm of the Spirit, in short, enables us to do justice *both* to the sovereign freedom *and* to the substantial reality of God's gift to men.

The language of grace and of faith is, of course, still relevant. It is possible to say "no" to God's gift of Himself in Jesus Christ. But there must be no *opposition* between personal and ontological categories, and above all we must see that, in terms of the Spirit, ontological categories are consistent with God's utter freedom. The language of faith and grace must be encompassed about, as it is in the New Testament, with the language of God's abiding and powerful presence in history, and with the knowledge that we are invited to become fellow-workers with His holy Spirit in the transformation of creation. It is hardly possible to resist the conclusion, indeed, that only the whole work of the Triune God in creation and redemption can properly be called "catholic", and that we apply this adjective to particular denominations, to particular formulations of the faith, and even to the whole Church on earth, in a derivative and secondary sense. It is in the light of this insight that we proceed to a discussion of what unity means, and of some of the considerations involved in trying to achieve it.

5

CATHOLICITY AND THE ACHIEVEMENT OF UNITY

WHAT PLACE has the effort to achieve unity in the midst of this discussion? Is unity a means or an end in the rediscovery of that fulness of God's work we call catholicity? How can the pursuit of unity be carried on in such a way that the real purposes of the ecumenical movement are accomplished? These are the questions which must occupy us in this closing chapter, for it is at the point of seeking unity with our fellow-Christians that the requirements of ecumenism become most sobering, immediate, and pressing.

Discussion of unity is bedevilled, of course, by confusion concerning the meaning of the word. Dr. Visser't Hooft has distinguished four senses in which the term is properly used: our given unity in Christ, our present and growing unity in the ecumenical movement, the churchly unity we seek to attain with each other, and the ultimate unity of the Una Sancta.[1] Here we are interested in the third sense of the term. Our concern is the very down-to-earth matter of actual union *negotiations* between churches. We cannot let this aspect of unity get out of focus because we have a theological interest in the other levels of the discussion. Rather we must bring whatever we can learn of what unity means in its less tangible forms to bear upon the actual policy issue: what are we going to do now about getting the churches together?

The interests of unity are best served, of course, by putting

See the formulation in *The Pressure of Our Common Calling*, pp. 87 ff.

union negotiations in a proper perspective. Unity is as much a matter of will as it is of theological ingenuity. If we want unity, we must mobilize entire churches to achieve this end. And if we do this, we must have convincing reasons *why* so much time and energy ought to be devoted to such ends, and how. Blind determination to push through a particular union at *any* cost can do as much damage to the life and witness of the Church as total lack of interest in our Christian neighbours. Just because the achievement of unity requires very great effort it is important not to waste energy and enthusiasm. It is important to know who must move, and when. It is essential that union discussions have the right place in the total activity of the Church, not draining resources from other legitimate functions, but rather strengthening Christian witness and Christian life wherever possible.

It is clear, from the start, for example, that the committee work necessary to devise plans of union is not the main function of the Body of Christ, but an auxiliary function designed to let the Church be the Church more fully. If organizational manœuvers in the interest of unity become an obsession, we may forget what we are seeking unity *for*. There are instances in which such loss of perspective has led to the formulation of faulty or inadequate union plans, to the isolation of those engaged in union efforts from the main bodies of the churches they serve, to misunderstanding, frustration, and failure that could have been avoided. Furthermore, a little perspective might sometimes save negotiators the self-righteous assumption that they alone are on the vanguard of the Church's life, and from so close an identification of some particular plan with their own egos that they cannot accept with good grace even those checks or surprises engineered by the Holy Spirit. It is a fact, in some instances, that after the failure of some given union plan the churches concerned have discovered still better ways of seeking union, and when this has been done without bitterness, the ecumenical cause has profited.

On the other hand, it is equally true that the theological work of an able union committee can be a source of renewal for the entire Church. Given the needed breadth of understanding on the part of the negotiators, the proper two-way lines of communication with the Church as a whole, and a realization on all sides that no aspect of Church life is not ultimately involved in the union effort, the very existence of such conversations can raise the sights of every person and every institution concerned. Even, indeed, if at a given point a union committee must say "no", there can be incalculable gains in life and understanding accruing from the very process of dialogue.

There is a still broader point of view, however, in terms of which each union discussion needs to be set in its proper place. In the statement on unity adopted by the Third Assembly of the World Council of Churches, it is clear that there are two poles of interest: Church unity in "each place" (by which is clearly meant unity that is visible in terms of the locality, geographical, sociological, or psychological, in which man meets his immediate neighbor), and recognition of this unity by "the whole Christian fellowship in all places and in all ages". In these two dimensions, the churches are called to acknowledge the work of the Holy Spirit in creating "one fully committed fellowship, holding the one apostolic faith, preaching the one gospel, breaking the one bread . . ." If one takes these words seriously, it is clear that no negotiating committee as such can claim to represent all the localities in which unity must be worked out: much less either "the whole Christian fellowship in all places and in all ages", or "the one apostolic faith . . ." In relation to such realities, the committee itself is a mere instrument with limited functions. Church union, for example, has to be *negotiated* at the same ecclesiastical level at which it is going to be *enacted*. This is usually the level of independent nationally organized "denominations." A union committee may well be an arena for the operation of the Holy Spirit, but in its actual functions it is still responsible to the negotiating churches and hence tied to the realities of an existing ecclesiastical situation. Lest this be lamented as a crippling drawback, let it be noted that this very limitation gives the union committee a definite, particular job to do, a definite function to which it can give its whole attention. That function is basically to draft an *enabling act* whereby the churches involved can move forward together to become what they really are. No union committee should be made to feel responsible for the whole ecclesiastical past or for the whole future of the Church. The task of the committee is to find a way in which the Church can live as one *now*, under such conditions that the treasures of the past can flow into the new forms which God has in store for His people.

In short, this means that unity of the kind that can be negotiated by committees is never an end in itself. Negotiated amalgamations cannot be simply identified with unities of which the creeds speak. We must not expect union negotiations to cure every sickness that afflicts the Church. If, perchance, a particular church union turns out to be mainly a matter of joining together two forms of ecclesiastical unfaithfulness, it is hard to imagine that the mere fact of union has any great value in the sight of God. But when union negotiation is part of a church-wide stirring of mind and energy, when it becomes the expression of a new sense of wholeness and purpose, then it ought to go on from strength to strength.

Furthermore, experience has shown that it is only when union talks are placed in a context of renewal that the technical problems of the discussion have any chance of real solution. By themselves, in the abstract, the theological antinomies that separate the churches are virtually insoluble. If the whole future of the Church is thought to rest only on the formulas a union committee may find, it is understandable that theologically sensitive persons may dig in their heels. But when it is evident that the union talks as such are only part of a tide of new insight and power that is sweeping over the Church, then the problems with which the negotiators must wrestle will often be transformed by being lifted to new levels of apprehension. This does not mean that the problems are ignored, or that in a haze of enthusiasm they come to seem less difficult. On the contrary, it means that problems are seen in their true dimensions, that false inferences are less frequently drawn, that ways forward begin to emerge in sharp relief.

Our discussion of the meaning of catholicity has provided some standpoints which may be of value in considering questions which union negotiators frequently meet. An attempt to apply these insights to union problems will test their value, as well as illustrate several aspects of their practical meaning. We will take up three problem areas in particular: those of "mutual recognition", of "intention", and of finding the way to "unify" separated ministries.

The Problem of Mutual Recognition

No union negotiation is long under way when it discovers what is in, effect, a "prior" question. Two or more churches propose to get together. The very fact that they propose this implies that in some sense they recognize each other as churches within the Una Sancta. Their common membership in ecumenical organizations such as the WCC already implies an undefined degree of mutual recognition, but the decision to open negotiations for unity makes it necessary to examine the meaning of this recognition with special care. It often appears that there are unsuspected problems lurking here at the very beginning of the road to unity: problems which, if they are not openly faced at the outset, can crop up later with devastating consequences. In the briefest way possible, and with the danger of oversimplification, it is the experience of many that mutual recognition is not something that can profitably be the subject of *negotiation*. It is something whose germinal existence has to be presupposed. It is something which must grow with growth in understanding. It is something which must be increasingly expressed in united action, and fully expressed with the consummation of unity itself. This point must be well understood by all concerned lest the discussion fall into lines that are bound to increase tension and misunderstanding rather than resolve them.

To make recognition a matter for negotiation is, in effect, for each side to demand that certain concessions, readjustments, or

D

theological subscriptions be made *as a condition* for entering upon or continuing discussion of unity. A church, for example, may suggest to another church that relations would be much easier if that other church were willing, short of union, to "take episcopacy into its system". Or, on the other hand, one church may demand that another church declare explicitly that it fully recognizes the former church's orders, sacraments and so on as a basis for further progress in union talks. To allow such a discussion to come into the open is to give the impression that churches are actually negotiating the question of their *being* as Christian Churches: that they suppose that they can grant the character of churchliness to those who fulfil certain conditions, or that they must demand that such a recognition *be* granted for the sake of their own self-esteem. Churches willing to do this show that they do not understand the meaning of God's new creation. A church can be the Church only through faith, and in the power of the Holy Spirit. This is something that cannot be negotiated. It is, rather, the basis of all possible negotiation.

That this is no theoretical problem is obvious from recent history. In 1959, the General Assembly of the Church of Scotland voted to reject the proposals of the *Report on Anglican-Presbyterian Relations* on the ground that this report "did not appear to acknowledge fully the catholicity of the ministerial orders" of the Church of Scotland.[1] This is to say that the Church of Scotland demanded an explicit statement of recognition from the Anglican side as a condition for continuing the talks. The purpose of the Report was to secure such adjustments in the structures of the four churches involved as would permit them fully to recognize each others' ministry and sacraments. Inasmuch as the existing non-recognition was principally on the Anglican side, the Report was read, rightly or wrongly, as a demand that Presbyterians adopt a form of episcopacy *as the ditioconn* of being recognized as part of the Church of Jesus Christ.

[1] Report of the committee on Inter-Church Relations to the General Assembly of the Church of Scotland, 1959.

But, despite defects in the Report, this deadlock was really the result of misunderstanding on both sides. A discussion centering on the question of recognition was allowed to develop when neither side, so far as knowledgeable people were concerned, had any intention of either denying recognition or demanding it in the first place. But the terms of the document none the less left the negotiating committee open to the charge that this was the case, and not enough preparation had been made on either side throughout the churches involved to help people see the real intentions of the negotiators. Indeed, had the place of mutual recognition in unity negotiations been clearer to the Committee itself, the Report might well have been modified by making *much more explicit* the fact that intercommunion was to begin the minute the churches involved declared their intention to seek modification of their structures, not after these modifications were in effect, and that the ultimate goal of the whole proceeding was real unity, not merely mutual acceptance. But the question of mutual recognition *did* arise, and in a form which proved disastrous for the negotiations at that particular stage.

The root of the difficulty was, and is, that the divided state of Christendom implies that we do not recognize each other even when we affirm with all our hearts that we do. And attempts to overcome disunity are bound to bring the painfulness of our separations into prominence in the course of negotiation even if they suppress these separations in the end. The fact that a negotiation is going on at all is evidence of the fact that mutual recognition is granted at least in the sense that all parties are regarded as *within* the Church Catholic.

And yet churches in union negotiations must never be asked to be unfaithful to what they regard as Christian truth, and their faithfulness may at times seem to imply a non-recognition of others. This leads to situations in which one church is not satisfied with the seemingly self-contradictory attitude of another. For example, an Anglican body may affirm that "Anglican Churches ought to be ready to recognize the Presbyterian Churches as true parts of the One, Holy, Catholic, and Apostolic

Church"[1] and yet continue to deny full recognition to Presbyterian celebrations of the Eucharist. To this situation the Presbyterian will often apply a logic that the Anglican does not. The Presbyterian will demand that the Anglican recognize him in terms acceptable to himself, forgetting that the Anglican has his own difficulties in reconciling his convictions concerning the Church Universal with his confidence in the catholicity of his own communion. The Anglican speaks in terms of the paradox of catholicity as it must be expressed in his particular tradition. Thus he says, in the same breath, that he regards Presbyterians as part of the Catholic Church, and yet that he must preserve his own convictions about ministerial orders. In fact, he will affirm that Presbyterians are part of the Catholic Church not in spite of Anglican convictions *but in terms of what those convictions fundamentally mean*. That there is a verbal contradiction here no one will deny. But the Anglican simply cannot say what he believes any more clearly, and he is completely sincere in uttering both parts of the seeming antinomy. The Presbyterian cannot ask any more than this, and if the Anglican is ready to negotiate on such a basis, the Presbyterian should rejoice.

But the Anglican must also be patient when the shoe is on the other foot. It is hard to imagine, at any rate, that the *way* in which Presbyterians recognize Anglicans is more acceptable to Anglicans than the usual form of Anglican recognition is to Presbyterians. At least this Presbyterian writer would imagine that Anglicans sometimes feel that Presbyterians receive them into the Church Universal without much understanding of what that Church really is. Anglicans (and others) must occasionally feel that they are recognized too lightly and in a fashion that is not wholly deserving of serious reciprocation. Indeed, it is possible to imagine that some Anglicans sincerely feel that the price of *accepting* the recognition of Presbyterians, and other groups espousing open communion, is to be forced to take their

[1] Report of the Lambeth Conference of 1958, S.P.C.K., London, 1958, § 2, p. 43.

own position too lightly. What good is it to be welcomed into the Una Sancta by a group that understands the meaning of participation in this reality quite differently from the way you do?

Thus it appears that it is sometimes as difficult for some churches to *accept* recognition from others as it is for them to *grant* such recognition. The heart of the problem is that while we do recognize each other as part of the one Church of Jesus Christ, the *terms* in which we are able to do so depend on our respective ecclesiastical positions. If union negotiators do not understand this fact, and then proceed to discuss mutual recognition, it is likely to appear that there are no grounds for continuing conversations at all. The cure, however, is basically simple. Every church engaged in union negotiation, every negotiating committee, has the responsibility for a certain amount of homework. Every church must realize that the question of recognizing other churches produces domestic theological problems which must be worked out before that church is really ready for negotiations. The problems to be met are basically those with which the preceding chapters of this book have been concerned. If this homework is properly done, no church will come to another with premature demands, nor will any church approach another with an inferiority complex which needs to be fed.

The Question of "Intention"

What has now been said leads on naturally to a further consideration of major importance. It has been maintained that the purpose of union discussions is not to negotiate our recognition of each other as within the Catholic Church. What is it then? It is to find ways in which we can actually come *to live together in one Church*.

This is more than an ecumenical truism. If it is our intention to make agreed arrangements, not for recognizing each other, not for reconciling different systems of doctrine and order, but for bringing into being one Church in which "all in each place" can live together, then that intention has a profound effect upon the whole course of union discussion. Fundamentally, this intention casts every question in the form: What is the kind of obedience God requires of us now? What is the shape of the one Church that is to be? Whatever topic is then examined by the union committee, whether it be episcopacy, the eldership, or some point of doctrine, the central question is not the validity of the thing as it has been possessed by each church separately but the part it can play as a common possession of all in one Church. Moreover, the way is also open for the negotiating churches to find and adopt forms of life which *none* of them have possessed before: forms which are the gifts of union itself, to which they acknowledge themselves called by the Spirit of God.

The word *intention* here is borrowed from the science of liturgics, where it signifies the conscious will of the Church that a sacrament or other ordinance *be* that which the words and actions of the rite imply, and that which the Church in all ages and times has intended by these words and actions. Without the proper intention, the sacrament is empty: for example, in St. Augustine's favorite example of children who mimic the sacrament of Baptism in their play. With right intention, however, even a defective celebration of the sacrament is taken up into God's purposes: precisely because intention is a way of receiving and appropriating the promises of God in present time. In negotiations for unity, an intention which keeps the fulness and organic wholeness of the one Church ever at the center of attention can bring something of the substance of God's gift of unity into the discussions, and into the relations between the churches, while conversations are still going on.

Intention should be stated, if possible, in very specific terms. A vague pronouncement about the "great church that is to be" will not have the power of a public statement by two or more churches that it is *their* firm intention to find a way to live together as one. A great deal of the difficulty and misunderstanding which followed the publication of the *Report on Anglican-Presbyterian Relations* came from uncertainty about the final goal envisioned by this document. It was clear that the object was a situation of "full communion" between a Church of Scotland

and a Church of England, both modified in polity in order to make such a relationship possible. But nothing was said in the report about relationships between Episcopalians and Presbyterians in Scotland, or between Presbyterians and Anglicans in England. Were these bodies to be united, in each case, into one Church, or were parallel episcopacies to exist, if only on a small scale, in both areas? It seemed, from the wording of the Report, that full intercommunion, rather than actual union, marked the limit of what was contemplated by the committee. Under these circumstances, it appeared that episcopacy was to be taken into the polity of the two Presbyterian churches not as a form of government agreed upon by all in a single united Church, but as a means of validating full communion between churches still divided. The difficulties raised by this situation have been most graphically pointed out by a bishop of the Church of England, Dr. J. A. T. Robinson:

> Along this line one soon gets to the position, not that if the Church is to be one it must be episcopal, but that if a Church is to be a Church at all it must have bishops. Episcopacy comes to be commended not as the source and symbol of unity but as a gimmick for validating sacraments—and this is what neither Presbyterians nor Methodists nor any other non-episcopal Church will stand or *ought to stand*.[1]

Whether or not unified episcopates in Scotland and England respectively would have evolved out of the proposals in the Report, it seems just to say that a basic mistake was made in not representing episcopacy as a form of government for one Church in each case. To have done so would have removed many of the Presbyterian objections that their ministries and sacraments were not properly recognized, and the attention of the Churches could have been directed forward towards what they together, under God, intended to be. Indeed, it could be argued along this line that actual union should precede every other kind of accommodation, in order to demonstrate most graphically the meaning of *intending* above all to be one Church. But a future intention,

[1] "Episcopacy and Intercommunion", in *On Being the Church in the World,* S.C.M. Press, London, 1960, p. 105. (Robinson's italics.)

clearly expressed and solemnly subscribed, can change the aspect of many things done first, as indeed the Report itself insists on the issue of intercommunion.

> A solemn resolve to achieve reconciliation and unity, accompanied or followed by decisive action with this end in view, would place the whole issue of intercommunion in a new light. This question has normally been discussed in terms either of existing separations or of a fully realized unity. But such a solemn resolve would give a new significance to common participation in the Holy Communion, the sacrament of reconciliation and unity.[1]

Here, in spite of the indefinitely expressed intention of the Anglican-Presbyterian document itself, is a principle worth closer attention than has usually been given it.

The theological significance of this principle derives, of course, from the fact that no sacrament or ordinance can be an act of the Church Catholic without such an intention. We affirm the catholic intention of baptism by baptizing persons into the Church Universal, not into our particular denomination. We have a similar view of the meaning of ordination. And when the Eucharist is celebrated, it is the Eucharist of the whole Church of all ages and places. Without this sense of catholicity, our sacraments would not be sacraments. In celebrating them, or in performing other solemn churchly acts, we look forward to the consummated, visible unity of the People of God, and pray that the Holy Spirit will provide us with that earnest of realized catholicity which can confer authenticity upon what we do in spite of our weakness and separation. When, therefore, we enter into a covenant to seek visible unity with another particular church, we are simply applying our awareness of the demands of catholicity to a particular churchly relationship. We are doing, theologically, what we do whenever we celebrate the sacrament, but we are doing it in a new awareness of our separated Christian neighbors. We are acknowledging that the moment we recognize our neighbors in Christ as neighbors, it is no longer possible

---

[1] The Report as printed in the *Report of the Inter-Church Relations Committee of the Church of Scotland*, May, 1958, p. 35.

to go on with our sacramental life as if they were not there. If we have not yet worked out an actual union, we are bound by the Holy Spirit to declare our solemn intention to move towards such a consummation. The authority which binds us and thrusts us forward towards our neighbors is identical with the authority by which we have lived as Christians ourselves.

If all this is true, then no declaration of ecumenical intention can leave the rest of our Church life unaffected. By such a declaration we call upon the Holy Spirit to vouchsafe us an earnest of the unity of the Communion of Saints just as we do when we pray for the Spirit to sanctify an act of baptism, ordination, or Holy Communion. If a declaration to seek unity has no consequences for our actual church practices, then that declaration is theologically empty. It would certainly seem that intercommunion, transcending, if necessary, every existing ecclesiastical barrier, and contradicting, if necessary, the divergent demands of different theological systems, would be the right token of seriousness in proclaiming an ecumenical, or catholic, intention. Such a step would *not* imply that we had abandoned our convictions. It would *not* imply that we had found ways of reconciling the contradictions in our own thought. It would *not* mean that we considered our ministries already unified, or our church systems merged into one. It *would* mean, however, that we had learned how to give positive theological content to the ecumenical interim in which we live. We would have gotten beyond the rigid necessity of thinking only in terms of "existing separations or of a fully realized unity".

There is no doubt that the achievement of intercommunion (as well as other expressions of growing unity in Christ) would make a tremendous difference in the atmosphere of subsequent negotiations. It would make impossible any serious charge that one denomination failed to regard another's sacraments or orders as within the Church Catholic. It would considerably mitigate strife over the meaning of different devices for unifying the ministry. Moreover, if intercommunion were understood in the essentially eschatological sense just outlined, there would be no excuse for regarding it as a *terminus ad quem*, for that would deny its whole meaning. Intercommunion taken as a token of ecumenical intention could not but be a force pressing towards the full realization of unity. Furthermore, the positive effects of clearly expressed ecumenical intention would no doubt spread to the discussion of other issues such as the meaning of episcopacy, the significance of the liturgy, and the theology of the Church as such. Discussion on this level, in fact, would surely bring the Churches near to the threshold of consummated organic unity itself.

The Act of Union

In all the discussion of union plans, of course, the greatest attention has been centered on the means by which churches actually take the step of becoming one. Obviously, if this step is not taken, all that has been said above is of no effect. But the very prominence of the actual act of union, and of the various devices by which it is proposed to carry it out, has tended to distort the discussion. It is as if Church union were *only* a matter of finding the most ingenious method of satisfying all concerned about the validity of ministerial orders within the united Church. Hopefully, the foregoing discussion has made it clear that what *leads* to the act of union is of major importance in determining what that act will mean to those who participate in it. The actual words and gestures by which the uniting churches are made one are a recognition, an endorsement, a consummation, of ties which already exist by the power of the Holy Spirit. Such words and gestures can have no magical power to bring into being a oneness which is not already given by God.

One can say more. The act of union between uniting churches has most commonly taken the form of a "unification of ministries". There is no inherent reason, however, why this particular concern should dominate the actual moment at which the union is consummated. In mergers not involving Anglicans or other churches of "catholic" policy, indeed, the act of union will have a different character altogether: principally because it will not involve an apparently liturgical action such as the laying-on of hands. The point, of course, is, that even if "unification of ministries" has a central place among the actions taken by the churches at the moment they unite, what actually takes place at such a moment is necessarily broader. It could be more accurately described as a "unification of disciplines". It is the moment at which the churches concerned actually begin to function as one church; the moment at which the constitution written for the united church takes effect; the moment at which all ministries begin to function within the same jurisdiction; the moment at which actual oneness is celebrated by a service of Holy Communion held under the authority of the church that has just come into being.

It is important to keep such considerations in mind in examining the words and actions proposed in various union plans for the "unification of ministries", for the whole theological context in which such unification takes place throws light on its proper meaning and form. Are ministries to be united, as in South India, by a simple declaration that the churches are one, and by the evolution of a single order of ministry in the united church over a period of years? Are they to be united as in the Ceylon Scheme, in a liturgical act performed by a previously unified episcopacy? Or are they to be united, as in the plan for North India and Pakistan, by a liturgical act done by episcopal and non-episcopal representatives of the uniting churches acting together?

The answer will depend to some extent on local circumstances. If, for example, churches of different denominational background do not coexist in the same districts because of previous parity agreements, an act of the South India type may suffice. If, on the other hand, the Anglicans with whom one has to deal are of a very Anglo-Catholic persuasion, a Ceylon type act of union may be needed. From this it is obvious, of course, that the writer does not believe that there is any single theologically mandatory device for consummating an act of union. Nor does he believe that there are any hard and fast rules about what churches of the Reformed tradition should permit their ministers to do, or forbid them to do, in a service of unification. There are three theological *principles*, however, which apply to all acts of union, and which ought to be equally acceptable to all parties whatever their churchmanship.

First, *the act of union must be understood as an action of the united church, not of the separated churches.* At first glance, this may seem a contradiction in terms, but it is a statement having important meaning. In the editions of the Plan for North India and Pakistan preceding the present (1957) one, a service of unification was proposed which made it apparent that the uniting churches would seek to confer some form of ministerial commission *on each other*, giving rise to the quip that this was a union plan in which "everybody lays hands on everybody else, and the Holy Spirit sorts out who does what to whom!" So long as one is in this position, the way is open for invidious distinctions: as, for example, between what Anglicans do to others and what others do to Anglicans. Moreover, an act of union of this kind would appear to ignore everything that has been said about mutual recognition and unitive intention as conditions *preceding* the formal consummation of the merger. Since 1957, the Plan for North India and Pakistan has happily abandoned this device in favor of a proposal that representatives of the uniting churches actually commission three ministers, one of whom is a bishop, *as the first ministers of the united church.* It is *these* three ministers who lay hands on all the other ministers, including the representatives of the uniting churches who commissioned them. Here it is made clear, by the very form of the act, that the united church itself commissions its ministers, and, indeed, subsequently consecrates or inducts its bishops. The union of the churches thus precedes the unification of the ministries, which is as it should be.

It will be said that this is an argument which depends on a certain amount of sophistry. But this is only so if the matter is examined *in abstracto*, apart from the actual situation in which the unification of ministries takes place. The act of unification is preceded by a solemn ratification of the constitution of the united church, so that this constitution is operative at the very moment hands are laid on the heads of those entering the ministry of this church. Furthermore, the act of unification is actually a *part* of a Communion Service, which is the first Eucharist to be celebrated under the discipline of the united church as such. When one considers the lengthy growing-together which the uniting churches will have shared if such a union is brought about, it is inconceivable that the act of union could be considered a mutual commissioning by these churches acting purely separately.

Ultimately, of course, to call the act of union the act of the united church is to speak in eschatological terms. The act is that of the united church because those who participate in it firmly believe that it is performed by the power of the Spirit which God is bestowing upon this church for its life from this moment forward. Thus, theologically speaking, there is little difference between a plan such as that proposed for North India and Pakistan and a plan of the South India type. Both see the operative factor in the united church's new life. The former consummates the unification of ministries at the start by an eschatological anticipation of what is to come. The latter allows the unification to be worked out in actual practice. The fact that in North India there is to be a specific ceremony of commissioning, while in South India there was not, does not change the fact that, in both, the united church is the reality which determines the meaning of the act and not the reverse.

The second principle is that *the act of union is an act with a definite meaning of its own distinct from ordination, reordination, or any other ecclesiastical ceremony performed by the separated churches in the past*. This is a point which is carefully guarded in the Plan for North India and Pakistan in these words:

> It is recognized that no name or title can be given to describe the nature of this service, as it has no historical precedent. The service is intended to be the means by which a new development in the restoration of the unity of the church is effected.[1]

[1] *Services Proposed for Use at the Inauguration of the Church of North India and the Church of Pakistan,* Second Edition, 1960, The Christian Literature Society, Madras, p. 23.

Some of the greatest difficulties in negotiating plans of union have arisen from attempts by certain of the participating churches to impose meanings satisfactory to them on the ceremonies laid down for the moment of union. Thus, the Convocation of Canterbury in 1961 voted to recognize and to enter into communion with the united church that would have been established by the implementation of the Ceylon Scheme

> provided the ambiguities in the rite of unification are removed so as to make clear that episcopal ordination is being conferred on those who have not already received it.

This, obviously, will not do. Any ceremony for the unification of ministries of course has, reasonably, to satisfy the parties to the union. But when one communion publicly calls for a particular interpretation to be given to the ceremony, when the actual plan of union carefully avoids spelling the matter out, trouble is bound to ensue. The North India Plan, for example, does not say that the formula for unifying the ministries is *not* ordination. But it never affirms that it is, and the words proposed for ordaining new ministers in the united church are quite different. A degree of latitude is left for the individual to satisfy his conscience as to what happens when the ministries are united at the time of union. This is the usual liturgical principle of leaving many strictly theological questions open while accomplishing the *deed* that needs to be done. But the appearance of an official statement concerning the act, designed to satisfy Anglican consciences in particular, greatly altered the situation in North India, for it made it appear that the formula for unification *was deliberately designed to be theologically ambiguous*, which is a very different thing from merely leaving theological questions open while the needed action is accomplished. This, more than anything else, has called forth doubts about the Plan, unfairly no doubt, but with very deleterious effect on the negotiation.

It is evidently not enough to say that the act of unification of the ministries "has no historical precedent", profoundly true as this may be. If this ceremony is not simply to be subject to the interpretation of the party with the most lively interest in placing an interpretation upon it, it must be given a definite meaning of its own. What meaning? Here one must tread softly, for sheer innovation can hardly be expected to solve problems such as this. But surely the act of laying-on hands with prayer is of ancient provenance in the Church, and not by any means exclusively associated with the initial induction of a man into lifetime ministerial status. More often, one suspects, this action was a prayer for and symbol of the renewal of the Church by the Holy Spirit, where members of the body took on some new ministry or responsibility. Why not say this and also use a similar liturgical act as a symbol of renewal in the united church *after* the union is accomplished? If the act by which the ministries of the church were originally united continued to be employed, in addition to ordination, when a minister took on a new charge or in other appropriate situations, the meaning of the original act of unification would be safeguarded and the primacy of the Holy Spirit in the life of the Church affirmed.

Thirdly, and finally, *the act of union should be understood not as a way of foreclosing certain alternatives for the visible life of the Church, but as a way of opening new possibilities*. When churches come together, there must be agreement that henceforth they will live under some particular system of church government. Otherwise there is no visible unity. But this must *not* be taken to mean that all theological questions about the structure of the Church are thereby settled. The achievement of unity does not "settle" arguments. It enables Christians to live together. The two things are very different.

It is evident at the outset, of course, that many united churches will in future be organized with an episcopal system of government. This will not be to say, however, that they are merely taking over the form of episcopacy that has existed in any given church up to that time. The very fact of union will make the episcopacy different in theory, in appearance, and in actual operation. There will be no decision here as to whether episcopacy is inherently superior to presbyterianism or congregationalism. There will, rather, be a decision that this is a useless argument altogether, and that Christ's Church must move on to new and better things. And, if this is the case, the united church will surely be free to adapt itself to the requirements of the gospel in any situation it may meet. It will be free because it has freely chosen the form of government which makes the union possible in the first place.

Sometimes it seems that we make the actual achievement of unity much too difficult, and, in consequence, consider the *continuing* theological work of the Church much too simple. After all, the real theological task lies not on this side of union but on the other side: when the Church is really in a position to face the world as the one Church of Jesus Christ. Then the truly churchly questions can be asked. Then the apologetic and evangelistic challenge will appear in its full immensity. Then the many possibilities for the life of the Church will be able to explored without denominational or confessional special pleading. If union is regarded as a simple capitulation of different churchly forms to one form, none of these possibilities can be grasped, and union is not worth having. But if the openness of the future which God has in store for His people can once be glimpsed, it will be impossible to think of union as either capitulation or victory again. It will only be possible to think of it as obedience to what the Holy Spirit, through all the ages, has been saying.